2/09   10 00

D0801707

MASSACHUSETTS

CONGREGATIONALIST

POLITICAL

THOUGHT

1760–1790

MASSACHUSETTS
CONGREGATIONALIST
POLITICAL
THOUGHT
1760–1790

the design of heaven

Dale S. Kuehne

UNIVERSITY OF MISSOURI PRESS
COLUMBIA & LONDON

5 4 3 2 1   00 99 98 97 96

Library of Congress Cataloging-in-Publication Data

Kuehne, Dale S., 1958–
    Massachusetts Congregationalist political thought, 1760–1790 : the
design of heaven / Dale S. Kuehne.
        p.   cm.
    Includes bibliographical references and index.
    ISBN 0-8262-1057-0 (alk. paper)
    1. Political science—United States—History—18th century.
    2. Puritans—Massachusetts—Clergy—History—18th century.
    3. Puritans—Massachusetts—Doctrines—History—18th century.
    I. Title.
JA84.U5K84   1996
320'.08'8258—dc20   96-7621
                                                                           CIP

∞™ This paper meets the requirements of
the American National Standard for Permanence of Paper
for Printed Library Materials, Z39.48, 1984.

Designer: Stacia Schaefer
Typesetter: BOOKCOMP
Printer and binder: Thomson-Shore, Inc.
Typefaces: Bodoni, Baskerville, Woodtype Ornaments

The University of Missouri Press gratefully acknowledges the support
of Saint Anselm College.

For credits, see page 181.

To my grandfather,
The Reverend Bert Robson Stanway

In this sense all power is from God, as that constitution, which makes government necessary, originates with him who is the author of nature; and such a constitution is as certain an intimation of the divine will, as an express revelation. There is no positive appointment or command; we argue the design of heaven that there should be civil government, because it is apparently for the advantage of mankind.

Andrew Eliot, 1765

CONTENTS

ACKNOWLEDGMENTS

This book is the result of the cooperation, sacrifice, and assistance of many people. My parents taught me the most important lesson by raising me to seek truth, wisdom, and knowledge, and making it possible to do so. My grandfather Bert Stanway modeled for me what it is to live truthfully. Mark Amstutz taught me the importance of religion and politics, Mulford Sibley taught me how to study it, R. Bruce Douglass forced me to do so rigorously, and James Skillen constantly testified that the effort was not in vain. Richard Lovelace guided me to the Puritans, and William Nigel Kerr was my guide to the Congregationalists. George Carey made my graduate education possible by agreeing to supervise and fund a student he did not know, on the basis of an incoherent eight-page paper. His optimism and labor in the midst of a life of infinite opportunities and demands provided yet additional testimony to the fact that the true measure of a professor is not merely knowledge and scholarship.

One of the most pleasant discoveries of my research was the encouragement and help many scholars offered freely. John Dunn, Bernard Bailyn, Carey McWilliams, and Donald Lutz made time to provide me with much helpful advice and encouragement. I was also privileged to have the assistance of some very talented students. Shannon Tole, Kurt Aubuchon, Andrew Rieger, and Robert Stouffer helped extensively, and I am grateful.

I received tremendous help from many libraries and librarians and I want to acknowledge them: Russ Pollard and the Andover-Harvard Library staff, the staff at the American Antiquarian Society, the Library of Congress, the staff at the Boston Athenaeum, Harold Worthley, and the Congregational Library. I wish to especially thank John Young, Elyse Fisher, and the staff of the William Jewell College Library, as well as Joe Constance and the staff of the Saint Anselm College Library for enduring countless special requests, interlibrary loan acquisitions, and overdue books. Their patience and cooperation are deeply appreciated. I also wish to recognize Beverly Jarrett, Jane Lago, and Julie Schroeder of the University of Missouri Press for their patience and professionalism.

Wisdom cannot be bought, but the pursuit of it can rarely be fulfilled without mammon. Father Peter Guerin and Saint Anselm College, Dean Jim Tanner and William Jewell College, Georgetown University, the

H. B. Earhart Foundation, and my extended family provided support crucial to various phases of my education and this project. The price of this endeavor, however, was not just dollars, but agape as well. James Gustafson dreamt with me and worked selflessly to realize the dream. Eleanor Gustafson prayed and then edited. My brother Ross edited and then prayed. For four years Ken Chatlos willingly and cheerfully deferred a sabbatical to Basel and spent time shielding me from administrative tasks that I might write. The sacrifice of Rachel, Naomi, Leah, and Ryan was even more profound, and it is to them I owe my deepest thanks.

MASSACHUSETTS

CONGREGATIONALIST

POLITICAL

THOUGHT

1760–1790

INTRODUCTION

Never before has so much been written with so little consequence.

John Dunn

These words, uttered in an unguarded moment, convey the frustration shared by many students of the American founding. Few subjects in the history of political thought have received more attention. Every extant work published in America prior to 1800 has been indexed and microfilmed,[1] and scholars continue to conduct substantial analyses of the political content of these writings, particularly of those written by the framers of either the Declaration of Independence or the Constitution. The intellectual ground of the founding is so well tilled that it is virtually impossible to find virgin soil. Nevertheless, the cultivating continues at a frenzied pace while an intense and often intractable debate on the meaning of the founding continues to rage.

Even though the research devoted to the founding is extensive, it remains an event worthy of attention. The character of the American founding is not just an academic historical topic; it holds ongoing significance for American politics. Understanding the nature of the founding is of critical importance for understanding the Constitution, its place in our tradition, and how we are to understand and apply its provisions today.

The importance of the founding, however, goes beyond public policy and jurisprudence. It is also "an integral part of [a society's] self-consciousness and the ultimate source of its sense of purpose and normative vision."[2] As John P. Diggins says:

> Classical political philosophers from Aristotle to the Founding Fathers to Hannah Arendt have insisted that for a constitutional republic to survive it must return to its first principles. The strength and future of a republic depends upon its capacity for periodic self-renewal through the reaffirmation of the pristine ideals that once inspired it. A republic

---

1. Charles Evans, comp., *American Bibliography: A Chronological Dictionary of All Books, Pamphlets and Periodical Publications Printed in the United States of America [1639–1800]*.

2. Steven M. Dworetz, *The Unvarnished Doctrine: Locke, Liberalism, and the American Revolution*, 3.

owes its meaning to the act of founding, to the historical "moment" of its creation.[3]

Consequently, the lack of consensus concerning the meaning of the American founding represents a profound threat to the ongoing viability of the Constitution and the nation. John Courtney Murray understood the consequences for a nation that cannot adequately answer questions concerning its self-identity:

> The very fact that these questions are being asked makes it sharply urgent that they be answered. What is at stake is America's understanding of itself. Self-understanding is the necessary condition of a sense of self-identity and self-confidence, whether in the case of an individual or in the case of a people. If the American people can no longer base this sense on naive assumptions of self-evidence, it is imperative that they find other more reasoned grounds for their essential affirmation that they are uniquely a people, uniquely a free society. Otherwise the peril is great. The complete loss of one's identity is, with all propriety of theological definition, hell. In diminished forms it is insanity. And it would not be well for the American giant to go lumbering about the world today, lost and mad.[4]

Clearly, understanding the founding is of such importance that further examination is warranted.

The Historiography of the Founding

John Dunn's frustration with the scholarly debate on the founding can be understood by examining its development since World War II. This debate has been chronicled in great detail by scholars such as Donald Lutz, Joyce Appleby, and Garrett Ward Sheldon, but a brief summary is important for introducing this examination of the founding.

Before World War II, the American Revolution and founding was considered chiefly a liberal event heavily influenced by John Locke.[5] This perspective was based primarily on the scholarship of Carl Becker and Louis Hartz. Becker, when analyzing the founding, discovered that

> so far as the "Fathers" were, before 1776, directly influenced by particular writers, the writers were English, and notably Locke. Most Americans had absorbed Locke's works as a kind of political gospel. . . .

3. John Patrick Diggins, *The Lost Soul of American Politics: Virtue, Self-Interest, and the Foundations of Liberalism,* 4.

4. John Courtney Murray, *We Hold These Truths: Catholic Reflections on the American Proposition,* 5–6.

5. Donald Lutz, *A Preface to American Political Theory,* 89–112; Joyce Appleby, *Liberalism and Republicanism in the Historical Imagination,* 11–17; Garrett Ward Sheldon, *The Political Philosophy of Thomas Jefferson,* 148–170.

If the philosophy of Locke seemed to Jefferson and his compatriots just "the common sense of the matter," it was not because Locke's argument was so lucid and cogent that it could be neither misunderstood nor refuted. . . . It was Locke's conclusion that seemed to the colonists sheer common sense, needing no argument at all. Locke did not need to convince the colonists because they were already convinced; and they were already convinced because they had long been living under governments which did, in a rough and ready way, conform to the kind of government for which Locke furnished a reasoned foundation.[6]

Hartz concurs with Becker. He finds that America is a nation "which begins with Locke, and thus transforms him, stays with Locke, by virtue of an absolute and irrational attachment it develops for him, and becomes as indifferent to the challenge of socialism in the later era as it was unfamiliar with the heritage of feudalism in the earlier one." "There has never been," he contends, "'a liberal movement' or a real 'liberal party' in America: we have only had the American Way of Life, a nationalist articulation of Locke which usually does not know that Locke himself is involved."[7]

Following World War II, however, the Lockean reading of the American founding was challenged by a number of scholars. What united those opposed to Becker and Hartz was the conviction that the Locke thesis is, at the very least, too simplistic, and at most, wholly inaccurate. Carolyn Robbins and others found evidence to suggest that the intellectual mix of the founding was broader than liberalism and Locke. Robbins demonstrated the importance of the English libertarian heritage to the intellectual climate of the founding and showed that "men such as Harrington, Milton, Sidney, Neville, Molesworth, and Trenchard and Gordon . . . had a central and continuing influence on early American political thought."[8]

Others, particularly John Dunn, questioned whether Locke should be considered an important influence in the politics of the Revolution and founding. Dunn argued that, contrary to the conventional wisdom on the founding, it did not appear that Locke was politically influential for the colonists. As evidence he cited the fact that the *Two Treatises* were "of no great popularity before 1750 and the tradition of political behaviour

6. Carl Becker, *The Declaration of Independence: A Study in the History of Political Ideas*, 27, 72–73.

7. Louis Hartz, *The Liberal Tradition in America: An Interpretation of American Political Thought since the Revolution*, 6, 11.

8. Lutz, *A Preface*, 94; Carolyn Robbins, *The Eighteenth-Century Commonwealthsman: Studies in the Transmission, Development, and Circumstance of English Liberal Thought from the Restoration of Charles II until the War with the Thirteen Colonies*; see also Jerome Huyler, *Locke in America: The Moral Philosophy of the Founding Era*, 6–7.

within which the colonists conceived their relationship with England was already highly articulated by this date in its most general values, though not of course in its specific understanding of the constitutional relationship." Moreover, Dunn cast considerable doubt on the frequently advanced arguments that Locke's "ideas were absorbed by a sort of intellectual osmosis, so that Americans could be of Locke's party without knowing it, rather as men earlier in the century could be Newtonians without having read a word of the *Principia*." "Tempting" though the analogy is, he regarded it as "spurious."

> The *Principia* achieved an immediate European pre-eminence. . . . The *Two Treatises* never enjoyed such an unchallenged European reputation. It was not even particularly widely known outside the English speaking world for eighty years after its composition and it became well known then only because of the huge influence of Locke's epistemology. . . . Above all it was only one work among a large group of other works which expounded the Whig theory of the revolution, and its prominence within this group is not noticeable until well after the general outlines of the interpretation had become consolidated.

Dunn concluded that Locke's influence had been so vastly overrated because it was "at least in part a product of the fact that [scholars] have read so little else of the English political writing contemporary with it."[9]

These and other studies so thoroughly devastated the conventional wisdom on the founding that since the mid-1960s there has been an explosion of revisionist scholarship reexamining American intellectual history during this era. Most of this examination focuses on republican thought. Bernard Bailyn, Gordon Wood, and J. G. A. Pocock, who wrote three of the most important revisionist works of the late 1960s and 1970s, all argue for the importance of republicanism.[10] According to Joyce Appleby, Bernard Bailyn's *The Ideological Origins of the American Revolution* introduced new parameters for the study of the American Revolution and brought republican theorizing into the academic mainstream,

> although curiously the word republicanism does not figure prominently in his text. . . . By joining earlier work on the English Commonwealthmen to a powerful explanation of how ideas enter into the realm

9. John Dunn, "The Politics of Locke in England and America in the Eighteenth Century," 79–80.

10. Bernard Bailyn, *The Ideological Origins of the American Revolution;* Gordon S. Wood, *The Creation of the American Republic, 1776–1787;* and J. G. A. Pocock, *The Machiavellian Moment: Florentine Political Thought and the Atlantic Republican Tradition.*

of history-making events, he made ideology the central concept in our current accounts of the break with Great Britain. . . .

It remained for Bailyn's student Gordon Wood to connect explicitly the conceptual order of the American patriots to the classical republican tradition in England. . . . Bailyn and Wood left unexamined the genesis of the English ideology they found flourishing in the colonies. Content to explore how classical republicanism organized the consciousness of the most influential generation in American history, they presented the source of the founders' ideology as a kind of grab bag of radical Whig notions about power, rights, and virtue. It was left to J. G. A. Pocock to provide a central nervous system for the new skeleton of American political culture which they had fashioned. And this he did in *The Machiavellian Moment*.[11]

In this work Pocock argues that the chief intellectual influence on the founding can be traced to the classical republican tradition as transported through the writings of the early-eighteenth-century British Whigs. According to this paradigm,

The idea of republicanism had its origin in classical antiquity, found its most profound political expression in Renaissance humanism, and culminated in certain aspects of the eighteenth-century Enlightenment. The moral exhortations of Cicero, the political theories of Machiavelli, and the constitutional devices of Montesquieu were its rich legacy. In republicanism true citizenship is founded upon the demands of "virtue," a political ideal whose realization required not only the people's direct participation in civic affairs but the subordination of their interests to the public good. A republic, however, is always threatened by its own impermanence, for the passage of time softened the citizenry's moral fibre, brought wealth and luxury, and, especially in English politics, undermined the austere, rural values of the "country" party, making it possible for the corruptions of the "court" party to prevail. . . . This inevitable process of corruption can be arrested only through the periodic revitalization that can be brought about by returning to original principles . . . and recapturing the concept of civic virtue.[12]

Pocock maintains that it is precisely this ideology that lies at the foundation of the American revolution.

In the first place, it has been established that a political culture took shape in the eighteenth-century colonies which possessed all the characteristics of neo-Harrington civic humanism. Anglophone civilization seems indeed to present the picture of a number of variants

11. Appleby, *Liberalism and Republicanism,* 280–82.
12. Diggins, *Lost Soul,* 10.

of this culture—English, Scottish, Anglo-Irish, New England, Pennsylvanian, and Virginian, to look no further—distributed around the Atlantic shores. The Whig canon and the neo-Harringtonians, Milton, Harrington and Sidney, Trenchard, Gordon and Bolingbroke, together with the Greek, Roman, and Renaissance masters of the tradition as far as Montesquieu, formed the authoritative literature of this culture.[13]

It is important to note that although Appleby is correct to point out the significance and connection of these three works, they, like republican scholarship in general, have different understandings of the origins and meaning of republicanism, as well as its particular importance to the founding. Pocock argues that a classically rooted republicanism was very important to the founding generation. Bailyn regards republicanism as an important part of a potpourri of various influences, and Wood discovers "a distinctively American republican theory—one that was not simply appropriated from European origins."[14] Hence, the republican paradigm, though exceedingly influential, is not monolithic.

Republicanism has not been the only focus of research for revisionist scholars. Others have identified the Scottish Enlightenment as another prominent source of influence at the founding. According to Lutz, the Scottish Enlightenment had three components: a theory of moral philosophy, a theory of economic progress, and a theory of history.[15] As a moral philosophy, the Scottish Enlightenment "challenged the Lockean conception of human nature by positing a naturally social being stimulated to care for others by a sense of sympathy and benevolence."[16] This moral philosophy lies at the heart of the Scottish Enlightenment's vision of economics and human history. The general economic welfare of society will best be promoted by allowing these social-minded and benevolent citizens to pursue their own self-interest, resulting in a material progress that will yield an ever increasing progress of liberty in history.[17]

The importance of Scottish philosophy to the American founding has been championed by, among others, Garry Wills. The focus of Wills's published scholarship is the Declaration of Independence and the *Federalist*

---

13. Pocock, *The Machiavellian Moment*, 506–7.
14. Lutz, *A Preface*, 100; see also Sheldon, *The Political Philosophy*, 152–53.
15. Lutz, *A Preface*, 124.
16. Sheldon, *The Political Philosophy*, 162.
17. Lutz, *A Preface*, 124–27.

Papers. In his first book, *Inventing America,* he argues that Thomas Jefferson's original version of the Declaration reflects the influence of Scottish common-sense thought that was deeply imbedded in him.

> The ideas expressed by Jefferson in 1776 were first introduced to him, and examined by him, in the prior decade of intense reading and discussion that formed his mind. . . . Those ideas were not derived, primarily, from Philadelphia or Paris, but from Aberdeen and Edinburgh and Glasgow. We have enough evidence of his reading, and of his conclusions from that reading, to establish that the real lost world of Thomas Jefferson was the . . . invigorating realm of the Scottish Enlightenment at its zenith.[18]

Yet Wills does not believe the influence of Scottish thought is limited to Jefferson. Rather, he holds that its influence on the founding is pervasive and can readily be seen in the *Federalist Papers* and the Constitution.[19] Although Wills does not attempt to eliminate the presence of Locke or republicanism from the founding, he finds Scottish thought to be of more importance and does not want its significance overlooked.

Wills is most often cited as the exponent of this position, yet he is hardly a lone voice. Forrest McDonald regards the influence of the Scottish Enlightenment as "obvious," and Thomas Pangle notes that, especially with respect to the *Federalist Papers,* "the strong influence of Hume was persuasively demonstrated by Parrington, Stourzh, and Adair, the latter of whom pointed out the likelihood of more general influences of Scottish thinkers on the Founders."[20]

Not all scholars, however, are persuaded that republicanism or the Scottish Enlightenment, either alone or in tandem, best explain the character of the founding. Some are revisiting the liberal thesis and finding that a more nuanced expression of it better explains the meaning of the founding. Although they acknowledge that the old orthodoxy was uncritical in its acceptance of liberalism and simplistic in its disregard for other influences, they assert that of all the ideas that impacted the founding, liberalism is primary.[21] As Isaac Kramnick states,

18. Garry Wills, *Inventing America: Jefferson's Declaration of Independence,* 180.
19. Garry Wills, *Explaining America: The Federalist.*
20. Forrest McDonald, *Novus Ordo Seclorum: The Intellectual Origins of the Constitution,* n. 55; Thomas L. Pangle, *The Spirit of Modern Republicanism: The Moral Vision of the American Founders and the Philosophy of Locke,* 37.
21. Dworetz, *Unvarnished Doctrine;* Pangle, *Spirit;* and Isaac Kramnick, *Republicanism and Bourgeois Radicalism: Political Ideology in Late Eighteenth-Century England and America.*

Republican revisionists must reconsider their judgment that late eighteenth-century political thought was engaged less by "Locke's concern with questions of obligation, original contract and natural rights than was originally thought to be the case." The revisionist assumption that ideas of mixed government, a balanced constitution, and separation of powers monopolized political discourse in the last half of the century at the expense of concern with the state of nature or the doctrine of consent must be revisited. The language of politics in late eighteenth-century England and America was about the origins of government as well as about the forms of government. It was about consent as well as civic virtue. It was about the social roots of magistrates as well as about the moral duties of magistrates.[22]

Not only are scholars reexamining the liberal interpretation of the founding, but many are finding that of all the various liberal influences, Locke is indeed dominant. Ronald Hamowy, for instance, in a critique of Wills argues that Locke was much more influential on Jefferson than the Scottish Enlightenment.[23] Thomas Pangle also argues vigorously for the priority of Locke.

It is not unreasonable to contend that Locke's influence on the eighteenth century, especially in America, was massive; but those caught up in the spiritual revolution he did so much to inspire—even the avant-garde of that revolution—probably did not always grasp the full meaning or momentum of the new theoretical currents he helped set in motion. One may rightly say that in the generations after Locke, lesser men of all stamps of opinion and sect felt increasingly the compulsion to explain their views using Lockean ideas. . . . By the late eighteenth century, the largely Lockean consensus on political first principles and on the relation between politics and religion was so strong that only a few articulate Americans still sensed a need to thrash out the deep doubts imbedded in the lingering legacies of biblical and classical thought.[24]

Although Steven Dworetz finds both republicanism and liberalism in the founding, he argues that liberalism is dominant because the only republicanism that exists is that which is in accord with Locke and liberalism. He asserts, "*American* republicanism in the revolutionary years was a distinctively *liberal* republicanism because it was embedded in a

22. Kramnick, *Republicanism*, 293–94.
23. Ronald Hamowy, "Jefferson and the Scottish Enlightenment: A Critique of Garry Wills's *Inventing America: Jefferson's Declaration of Independence.*"
24. Pangle, *Spirit*, 126.

political and intellectual tradition which included a vital and essential Lockean-liberal component."[25]

Even though the revisionist movement has greatly enriched our understanding of the founding, there are still others who argue that the concentration on philosophical sources has caused scholars to overlook the most important source of American political thinking of this era: Protestant Christianity. Barry Alan Shain is one of a number of scholars who argue for the importance of Protestantism in the founding.

Protestant ideas

> After having been introduced in the early 1980s to the revisionist historiography of republicanism, I experienced something approaching an epiphany and began to conduct my research. I expected that republicanism, with its particular intellectual contours, would prove congenial to someone like me, since I had been deeply influenced by the activist democratic aspirations of 1960s radical politics. . . .
>
> Although I was not disappointed in my search for a communal American past, my endeavor to discover a noble and powerful secular republican one was fruitless. The Revolutionary-era intellectual foundations that I uncovered proved to be less classical or Renaissance republican and more Calvinist (or reformed Protestant) than I had anticipated.[26]

John Diggins is another. In his research, Diggins discovered that Protestant Christianity, and Calvinism in particular, is of greater importance than even liberalism. He contends that Calvinism is the forgotten intellectual source of both liberalism and the founding, and that to ignore the Calvinism inherent in both is to misunderstand both.

Calvin

> In studying American liberalism, most historians have focused almost solely on political ideas and have therefore slighted the religious convictions that often undergird them, especially the Calvinist convictions that Locke himself held: resistance to tyranny, original sin and the corruptibility of man, labor and the "calling" as a means to salvation, and the problem of man's infinite and insatiable desires, which compel him to be in "constant pursuit" of happiness.[27]

Diggins suggests that Calvinist Christianity was one of the most important influences on the intellectual life of eighteenth-century America and, because this element no longer characterizes American thought, scholars

25. Dworetz, *Unvarnished Doctrine,* 191.
26. Barry Alan Shain, *The Myth of American Individualism: The Protestant Origins of American Political Thought,* xv.
27. Diggins, *Lost Soul,* 7.

have tended to overlook its past contribution. Diggins believes that this error must be overcome if scholars are ever to establish a coherent and persuasive interpretation of the founding.

Shain and Diggins are not alone. Wilson Carey McWilliams calls the Bible "the second voice in the grand dialogue of American political culture, an alternative to the 'liberal tradition' set in the deepest foundations of American life." Alan Heimert argues in *Religion and the American Mind* that the Calvinist "New Light" theology that fueled the Great Awakening is the intellectual engine that powered the Revolution. He finds that although liberalism may have provided the intellectual justification for revolution, it was this particular form of Christianity that provided the motivation to revolt. "It was the more orthodox clergyman of America who infused the Lockean vocabulary with a moral significance, a severity and an urgency, and thereby translated the ideas of social contract and natural law into a spur to popular activity."[28]

Many fundamentalist Christians go beyond Diggins, McWilliams, and Heimert by arguing in the strongest terms for the intellectual primacy of reformed Christianity at the founding. Benjamin Hart, for example, argues,

> There has been a concentrated attempt in American academic circles to recast the Christian-based American Revolution in the image of the virulently anti-Christian French Revolution, which predictably ended in tyranny. Liberation of the individual was not an idea of the *philosophes;* it was a Christian idea, and specifically a Reformation idea, as America was settled overwhelmingly by fundamentalist Protestants.[29]

Our understanding of the founding has greatly deepened and matured since World War II, yet all is not well with the discipline. Although the new scholarship has clearly advanced our knowledge, what Dunn and other students of American history and political thought find so

28. Wilson Carey McWilliams, "The Bible in the American Political Tradition," 22; see also Lutz, *A Preface,* 136; and Jon Pahl, *Paradox Lost: Free Will and Political Liberty in American Culture, 1630–1760.* Alan Heimert, *Religion and the American Mind: From the Great Awakening to the Revolution,* 17; see also William G. McLoughlin, "Enthusiasm for Liberty: The Great Awakening as the Key to the Revolution."
29. Benjamin Hart, *Faith and Freedom: The Christian Roots of American Liberty,* 28; see also John W. Whitehead, *The Second American Revolution.* For an evangelical rebuttal, see Mark A. Noll, Nathan O. Hatch, and George M. Marsden, *The Search for Christian America.* For an evenhanded discussion of the fundamentalist/evangelical/mainline debate, see Jerry S. Herbert, ed., *America, Christian or Secular? Readings in American Christian History and Civil Religion.*

exasperating and discouraging is the hostile tenor and intractability of the scholarly discourse. For example, J. G. A. Pocock and Isaac Kramnick, two key leaders in the field, spare no words in their disagreement and their disrespect for the arguments of the other.[30] The literature is filled with scholarly disputes and assaults on character and integrity, masked in scholarly terms. Such digressions do little to advance the scholarly enterprise. Rather, the positions harden and the diatribes continue. Hope fades that there will ever be the cooperative effort needed to synthesize existing research and develop an understanding that reaches beyond our current intellectual horizon. Robert Shalhope summarizes the present situation:

> The extraordinary promise of recent research on republicanism for furthering our understanding of early America has not been fully realized. By exaggerating differences and obscuring potentially common ground, constant bickering between "ideological" historians and "social" historians has proven counterproductive. . . . Constant sniping between the two camps has prevented useful questions regarding republicanism's role in early American society from being asked, much less being answered.[31]

Methodology, Historiography, and the Founding

Nevertheless, there is still reason for hope. Our understanding of the founding has advanced significantly in the past three decades, and there is reason to believe that the stalemate between proponents of the various paradigms can be broken. The primary cause of the present stalemate is methodological. In their haste to arrive at a definitive understanding of the American founding, scholars have advanced claims concerning the meaning of the founding that are beyond what their research can justify.

The classical republicans, for example, often claim or imply that they have discovered the intellectual paradigm that governed the founding era. They believe we should gauge intellectual influence through an understanding of the socially constructed intellectual framework in which thinking takes place. They argue that every era has such a framework, and that this framework constitutes an ideology that forms the lens through which people understand the world. Hence, the key for understanding

30. Kramnick, *Republicanism*, 37; J. G. A. Pocock, *Virtue, Commerce, and History: Essays on Political Thought and History, Chiefly in the Eighteenth Century.*
31. Robert E. Shalhope, "Republicanism and Early American Historiography," 354–55.

the founding rests in understanding the ideological framework of the founding era. Accordingly, though various liberal, Christian, or Scottish ideas were discussed during the founding, the founders adopted only those ideas that cohered with their ideology. Consequently, if, as the classical republicans suggest, the ideology of late-eighteenth-century America is classical republican, then classical republicanism constitutes the essence of American political thought at the founding, and not liberalism, Calvinism, Scottish common-sense philosophy, or any other paradigm.[32]

The republican theorists are correct to emphasize the importance of context and ideology for understanding historical documents and their authors. Earlier scholars drew simplistic conclusions, and the republican theorists, particularly Pocock, have exposed their shallowness, greatly advancing our understanding of the founding. As Appleby points out:

> The sweep of Pocock's revision is breathtaking. Against the pull of two centuries of unexamined assumptions about the reception of economic progress, he has succeeded in giving us eighteenth-century men firmly planted in their own time, facing an uncertain future with the sensibilities of their predecessors in the foreground and the values of their descendants properly out of sight.[33]

The republican theorists are not alone in their contribution. All of the existing scholarship has enriched our understanding of the founding. However, in our haste to arrive at a more sophisticated understanding of the founding, scholars have advanced claims that move beyond the ability of their research to support. In their impatience to conclude the matter, they make generalizations or sweeping assertions about the meaning of the founding, while their evidence only supports more qualified or partial assessments. Garry Wills, for instance, apparently argued for the priority of Scottish common-sense philosophy before finishing his research. The book Wills intended to write on the Constitution, "Building America," was never published, but his general thesis requires the evidence this book would provide.

Pocock has given us new insight into the character of the founding and a methodology with which to study it, yet he and his disciples exaggerate republicanism's importance when they claim to have uncovered the meaning of the founding. As Appleby points out:

32. Appleby, *Liberalism and Republicanism*, 277–90.
33. Ibid., 284.

neither seventeenth-century England nor eighteenth-century America were tightly knit or cohesive societies. The high level of literacy in both countries encouraged the free circulation of printed material. Neither censorship nor limited access to printing presses existed to inhibit the publication of divergent, even inflammatory, points of view. . . . Both countries were intellectually as well as culturally pluralistic. The conceptual world of the elite permeated all classes, but it could not and did not exclude competing views—views which in time exercised greater interpretive powers for those differently positioned in society.[34]

Yet republican theorists are not alone; any scholar or paradigm claiming to explain the meaning of the founding is, at the least, premature and unwise. Given the amount of political writing that took place throughout the colonies, and the geographical and intellectual diversity of the nation at this time, it is not surprising that scholars have been able to identify a wide variety of intellectually significant threads in the founding. Thomas Jefferson himself recognized this and acknowledged it when writing to his fellow scholar and statesman, Henry Lee. He argued that the purpose of the Declaration was

> not to find out new principles, or new arguments, never before thought of, not merely to say things which had never been said before. . . . [I]t was intended to be an expression of the American mind, and to give to that expression the proper tone and spirit called for by the occasion. All its authority rests then on harmonizing sentiments of the day, whether expressed in conversation, in letters, printed essays, or in the elementary books of public right, as Aristotle, Cicero, Locke, Sidney, &c.[35]

America at the founding was no more monolithic than it is today. To speak of the intellectual meaning of America in any century means to speak of an intricate set of interrelated and independent ideas woven together in a complex manner. American political theory during the founding clearly drew from a number of varying influences, contexts, groups, and individuals from inside and outside the political elite. The framers of the Declaration and the Constitution are certainly an influential group worthy of study, but American political thought was not designed in its entirety by Jefferson, Hamilton, and Madison. Rather, it was conceived in the context of an already long and deep American political tradition and shaped by a political climate created by no single individual, group, or ideology.

34. Ibid., 286–87.
35. Thomas Jefferson, *Writings,* 1501.

It is premature to speak authoritatively about the meaning of the founding because our research remains incomplete. Most scholarship on the founding has focused on the political elite, key political individuals involved in the movement toward independence, or on those who drafted and defended the Constitution. This is the proper place to begin, and we now have profound insight into the minds of these individuals. American political theory, however, is broader and deeper than the political thought of the "framers." Madison's notes on the Constitutional convention reveal that the Constitution was not constructed by a few individuals ex nihilo but was assembled within constraints imposed on the delegates by the various constituencies they represented.[36] As Donald Lutz points out, the Constitution of 1787 in and of itself is incomplete.

> Obviously, the United States Constitution assumes, in fact requires, the existence of state constitutions if it is to make any sense. They are part of the national document and are needed to complete the legal text. The Framers, regardless of their attitude, had no choice but to recognize the brute fact of the existence of state governments.[37]

Many scholars, in their haste to pronounce authoritatively about the meaning of the founding, have overlooked the essential fact that the Declaration, the Constitution, and their authors are not the only politically significant documents and individuals. It appears that too much scholarly attention has been given to the political elite and too little to other groups and individuals that constituted America. Such imbalance is the primary cause of the academic impasse that plagues the discipline. To understand the American founding fully, we need to explore new domains, including the theory embodied in state constitutions, the political thinking of other political leaders who contributed so much to the contours of state politics, as well as the historically silent mass of citizens.[38]

Fortunately, whole new areas of study have emerged that complement the work that has been done on ideology and the political elite. One such area is social history. Recognizing that American political theory formed in a context where elites were accountable to and limited by the masses, social historians have sought "to reconstruct the lives of the many

36. James Madison, *Notes of Debates in the Federal Convention of 1787.*
37. Donald S. Lutz, *The Origins of American Constitutionalism,* 96.
38. See M. E. Bradford, *"Against the Barbarians" and Other Reflections on Familiar Themes,* which examines the substratum of leadership in America at the founding on the state level.

people who are without an explicit historical voice."[39] Another such area
is work done on the "political class." The phrase, coined by Donald Lutz,
describes the non-elite but politically active class of citizens that constitute
between 15 and 20 percent of the adult population.

> From this political class are drawn most of those people who con-
> sistently vote in every election, almost all of those who contribute to
> election campaigns, and virtually all of those who work for political
> parties, run for office, work for candidates whether partisan or non-
> partisan, organize and work for political-interest groups, write letters
> to newspapers and governmental officials, testify before governmental
> bodies, and write political essays for public consumption. These are the
> opinion leaders who immerse themselves in information about issues,
> candidates, and policies, and therefore the rest of the population looks
> to them for cues when deciding how to think about political matters,
> what opinions to hold, and how to vote.[40]

For Lutz, understanding the political writing of the "political class" may
be of greater importance than all the work that has been done heretofore
on the political elite.

> If a people are self-governing and their self-government is embodied
> in an evolving set of public documents that rests upon their consent,
> then it would seem perverse to focus American political theory upon
> a study of writings by a tiny elite. A portion of the population plays
> a disproportionate role in the design, operation, and analysis of the
> American political system. Far too numerous to be called an elite, the
> political activist class interprets and organizes politics for the rest of
> the population and interprets and organizes the needs and demands
> of the broader population for presentation to those in government.[41]

These two avenues of scholarly inquiry, social history and research
into the political class, are providing valuable information that comple-
ments the good work being done with political elites and ideology. When
combined, these approaches promise to yield the information necessary
to break the impasse and propel us to a deeper and more complete
understanding of the founding era.

The study presented here is an examination and explication of the
political thought of the Massachusetts Congregationalist clergy from 1760
to 1790, an important component of the Massachusetts political class
during the founding era. The clergy was the single most educated and

39. Lutz, *A Preface,* 101.
40. Ibid., 102–3.
41. Ibid., 152.

respected group in revolutionary Massachusetts. Congregationalism was the established religion, and the commonwealth was divided into parishes with the Congregational church functioning as the spiritual and political center of each parish. The Sunday worship services were the primary social activity of parish life and the most effective means of disseminating news and education throughout the colony, and town meetings were usually conducted in the church building.

The minister, as the most educated and visible person in the parish, held a position of considerable influence and frequently used it for political ends. Massachusetts was consistently a focal point of revolutionary activity, and the Congregationalist ministers were active participants. As Harry S. Stout discovered:

> From the repeal of the Stamp Act on, New England's Congregationalist ministers played a leading role in fomenting sentiments of resistance and, after 1774, open rebellion. Historians who minimize the clergy's determinative role in shaping New England's revolutionary mentality, pointing out that they drafted no official resolutions in their associations, miss the points at which the ministers made their vital contributions. Ministers' names pepper local records in a bewildering array of contexts: as town clerks, committee advisors, newspaper contributors, militia chaplains, and even militia commanders.[42]

Samuel Cooper, for instance, a Boston Congregationalist minister, was regarded during the founding era as the political equal of John Hancock and John and Samuel Adams.[43]

Not only did the ministers participate in the Revolution, they also engaged in the formation of revolutionary political thought. Given their educational background and theological concern for all aspects of human life, the Congregationalist ministers were expected to instruct their parishioners in topics ranging from the interpretation of current events to the meaning of life. When events required political thought and action, the ministers responded with an explosion of political sermons issued from pulpit and press. "By 1776, Congregationalist ministers in New England were delivering over two thousand discourses a week and publishing them at an unprecedented rate that outnumbered secular pamphlets (from all the colonies) by a ratio of more than four to one."[44]

42. Harry S. Stout, *The New England Soul: Preaching and Religious Culture in Colonial New England,* 283.
43. Charles W. Akers, *The Divine Politician: Samuel Cooper and the American Revolution in Boston,* 1.
44. Stout, *New England Soul,* 6.

The Massachusetts Congregationalist ministers were important members of the political class; because of their influence, their political theory is worthy of study.

The political importance of the Massachusetts clergy has not been wholly ignored by scholars. Puritanism, the theological parent of Congregationalism, has for decades been the focus of much attention by historians and political theorists. Forrest McDonald, Wilson Carey McWilliams, and others have all testified to the important contribution the Puritans made to American politics and the founding.[45]

Alice M. Baldwin's 1928 study, *The New England Clergy and the American Revolution,* was the first and, until now, the only comprehensive study of the political theory of the New England clergy. For decades, scholars have heavily utilized Baldwin's book, regarding it as the definitive work on the subject.[46] Although Baldwin's work is useful, it is dated and in need of revision. First, it lacks depth. In 172 pages she examines the political philosophy *and* political activities of the whole New England clergy during the first seventy-six years of the eighteenth century. Second, her conclusions need updating. Written decades before the historiographical revolution of the 1960s, the analysis lacks precision and reflects the uncritical assumptions of pre–World War II historiography. Exhibiting the scholarship of her era, Baldwin holds that Lockean liberalism constitutes the primary intellectual basis of the New England clergy's political thought and the politics of New England. Though these conclusions may be valid, they warrant reexamination.

Although her work is the only comprehensive treatment of the topic, the scholarship of others relates to our examination of this topic. One such work is Martha Louise Counts's 1956 Columbia University doctoral dissertation, "The Political Views of Eighteenth-Century New England Clergy as Expressed in Their Election Sermons." Like Baldwin's work, it contributes to our knowledge of the clergy's political thought, but its scope is too limited and its methodology too dated to be of more than limited usefulness in studying our intellectual heritage. Only election sermons are analyzed, thus leaving out political insights provided by the full range of the clergy's published sermons and miscellaneous writing. In

45. McDonald, *Novus Ordo Seculorum;* Wilson Carey McWilliams, *The Idea of Fraternity in America.*
46. Pangle, *Spirit;* Dworetz, *Unvarnished Doctrine;* and Nathan O. Hatch, *The Sacred Cause of Liberty: Republican Thought and the Millennium in Revolutionary New England.*

addition, the political theory is examined in such summary fashion that it is difficult to identify and differentiate between intellectual traditions that our present scholarly conversation requires.

We now require a study designed and conducted with enough precision so that it can provide meaningful information concerning the intellectual roots of the founding era. Most recent studies of sermons from the founding are broadly designed to introduce the reader to the field. Such studies are valuable but of limited usefulness in thinking deeply about intellectual roots. One example of this is Ellis Sandoz's introductory essay to his collection of colonial and revolutionary sermons. Although his research fulfills its purpose—introducing us to the political thinking of the revolutionary clergy and making available an abundance of important information and insight—its usefulness for commenting in a precise way about the intellectual heritage of the founding is limited. Since he digests the whole corpus of sermons and fails to distinguish the various philosophical and theological differences between the clergy members he is studying, he has difficulty entering into a nuanced discussion of their intellectual heritage. Although a Massachusetts Congregationalist, a New York Presbyterian, a Pennsylvanian Quaker, and a Virginian Anglican may all use the word *liberty,* the meaning of the idea may differ significantly. Treating them as one group, as Sandoz does, limits the depth of conclusions that may be drawn. Since scholars have done a good job in the last quarter century identifying the various threads of American political thought and the extent to which they were held, the present need is to conduct research with a narrower and more coherent focus.[47]

This study seeks to fill that need. It is more precisely focused than Baldwin's. Rather than examine the political thinking of all New England clergy in the eighteenth century, it examines the political thinking of the Massachusetts Congregationalist clergy from 1760 to 1790 as represented in its members' published writings. New England is a useful area of focus when discussing the seventeenth century, but the increasing diversity of New England as the eighteenth century progressed lessens its usefulness as a category. During this era Massachusetts Congregationalism developed a unique character and personality. It was at this time that the Saybrook Platform separated those in Massachusetts from their Connecticut brothers, resulting in Massachusetts's developing a different brand of

---

47. Ellis Sandoz, ed., *Political Sermons of the American Founding Era, 1730–1805;* see also Ellis Sandoz, *A Government of Laws: Political Theory, Religion, and the American Founding.*

Congregationalism. One source of this growing diversity was the different developments at Harvard and Yale. The two schools went in different intellectual directions in the eighteenth century, creating additional divisions between Massachusetts and Connecticut Congregationalists.

Other benefits of limiting this study to the Massachusetts clergy include the intellectual homogeneity of the group and the opportunity this unity gives us to more precisely understand its members' intellectual world. As almost all of them were Harvard graduates, they had a shared educational background. Also, the ministers were linked through membership in the Massachusetts Convention of Congregational Ministers, an organization with authority to speak for its members.[48] While the convention did not issue formal statements on political issues, it did have power to question or censure members who deviated too much from acceptable thought.

In addition to narrowing Baldwin's scope of ministers, this study also limits the time frame. The period from 1760 to 1790 is broad enough to include the founding era, yet narrow enough to draw meaningful conclusions about intellectual roots. An expanded time frame would involve examining the educational and intellectual backgrounds of a greater number of clergy and make the task of drawing useful conclusions more difficult because of the greater variety of intellectual influences that must be admitted to the study. Moreover, the narrower time frame provides a glimpse into the political thought of these ministers prior to the generally accepted beginning of the revolutionary period in 1763, allowing us to document changes that took place during the dynamic time in which America was transformed from colony to nation.

Having thus narrowed the scope, an approach must be developed to explicate the political theory of these ministers. It is important that we do our best to understand what their writing meant to those who wrote it, read it, and, in the case of sermons, heard it. The difficulty we encounter is that nowhere do the ministers ever state their political theory in a comprehensive manner, and only rarely do they devote their entire attention to politics, even in an election sermon. As a result we will have to go beyond the texts in order to fully comprehend their political thought.

This study will first examine the clergy's intellectual and historical background and context. Part I provides the overview necessary to illuminate the textual examination conducted in Part II. Part II includes an

48. Harold Field Worthley, "An Historical Essay: The Massachusetts Convention of Congregational Ministers."

analysis of the clergy's understanding of popular sovereignty, majority rule, rights, equality, the common good, political virtue, church/state relations, liberty, and institutional design. Such an examination will illuminate the clergy's response to a host of fundamental political questions.

The vast majority of the clergy's published political work consists of sermons. While only "partial" in nature, sermons are an especially rich source of political thinking, not only because they are the primary medium used by the clergy members to express their thoughts, but also because they represent ideas that were presented to virtually all citizens of Massachusetts.

> If we assent to the claims of recent scholarship that the colonial sermon was the "central ritual" of the culture, the key mode (and medium) of communication informing all levels of society, if we believe that the minister himself "embodied and expressed" the leading ideas of the culture, then we may observe, perhaps even enter, the world of revolutionary New England through the sermonic efforts of the patriot clergy.[49]

Consequently, this study has the potential of providing us with a rare picture of one portion of American political thought. Along with elucidating the political thought of the clergy, it will provide a glimpse of what the "silent" political masses heard, as well as how the thinking of the political elite was tempered and altered by the clergy.

Although this study focuses on sermons, other important sources of information are not ignored. Some ministers, such as Samuel Cooper, wrote letters concerning politics; others, such as Joseph Lathrop and John Cleaveland, wrote anonymous political tracts; and others made diary entries that were consulted and used as appropriate.

Those who have worked with eighteenth-century texts are aware that, by contemporary standards, spelling is inadequate. The writing of the Congregationalists is no exception. However, rather than acknowledging every misspelling in an eighteenth-century text with *sic,* I have decided to allow these texts to stand as much as possible on their own.

This study takes full advantage of the considerable resources provided by theologians, philosophers, and historians, and it does so without apology. Two studies of particular usefulness for this inquiry have been produced by historians and must be acknowledged. The first, *The Sacred Cause of Liberty,* is Nathan Hatch's fine study of republican and millennial

---

49. Donald Weber, *Rhetoric and History in Revolutionary New England,* 150.

themes in revolutionary New England. The second work of note is Harry Stout's *The New England Soul,* a monumental study of preaching and culture in colonial New England. One cannot research this topic without drawing on the scholarship of both Hatch and Stout. If political theorists are to advance the intellectual discourse of our discipline, we will have to draw more heavily on the insights of scholars from all fields.

Part I

THE

MINISTERS

AND

THEIR

WORLD

INTRODUCTION TO PART I

To discover the meaning of any utterance demands what is in substance a continuing act of literary interpretation, for the language with which an idea is presented, and the imaginative universe by which it is surrounded, often tells us more of an author's meaning and intention than his declarative propositions. An understanding of the significance of any idea, or of a constellation of ideas, requires an awareness of the context of institutions and events out of which thought emerged, and with which it strove to come to terms. But full apprehension depends finally on reading, not between the lines but, as it were, through and beyond them.

Alan Heimert

A thing worth doing is worth doing badly.

G. K. Chesterton

Interpreting documents over two centuries old requires an understanding of their context: the authors, the medium, the culture, the history, and the ideas on which they are based. Only then can we speak with any confidence about their meaning.

One of the overall purposes of this study is to identify and explicate the various intellectual traditions contained in the clergy's political thinking. Part I will examine intellectual traditions influential during the founding era. Providing adequate definitions for these traditions is essential for drawing adequate conclusions. Donald Lutz provides significant help in this area.

In his *Preface to American Political Theory,* Lutz identifies six "intellectual strands used by the founders to weave American political thought during the eighteenth century." The first he labels "Experience Must Be Our Guide." Lutz argues that "the most fundamental aspect of both Federalist and Antifederalist thought" was "the conviction that as useful as books can be, politics should always rest upon a base of human experience rather than upon logical abstractions, no matter how appealing or moral the abstractions." He further asserts that the colonists found three components

25

of experience persuasive: First, "the cumulative experience on American shores prior to 1776; the second was the insight that the Federalists had personally and directly gained during their" lives; and third, human history, especially the history of England.

The second category is called "The Republican Tradition." Lutz, however, finds that the founding generation did not have a commonly held meaning of *republican*. Lutz identifies four definitions from the era: First is "a traditional Whig position that equates republicanism with representation" and tacit consent. Second is a radical Whig definition that "emphasized popular sovereignty with direct, active consent as the basis of all facets of government—direct in the sense that the people gave it themselves and active in that their consent was required frequently," and modes of participation in addition to elections. Third is a Jeffersonian notion that abandoned representation in favor of more direct democracy, and fourth is Madison's view "that popular sovereignty only requires the people to rule in an ultimate sense through their approval of the Constitution."

Lutz's third category is "Lawyers and Liberals." Here he refers, first, to the influence of the English Common Law tradition particularly through Sir Edward Coke and Sir William Blackstone. Second, Lutz refers to what has come to be known as liberalism, particularly the "synthesis of concepts of social compact, consent, individualism, and political equality."

Lutz's approach is particularly helpful in trying to distinguish between republican and liberal thought. He makes the important point that

> the distinction between liberalism and republicanism that we might make today was not made in the eighteenth century, since, among other factors, the words "liberal" and "liberalism" had not yet been used to describe political ideas. "Republic," on the other hand, was very much in use by Americans after 1776, even though "republicanism" as a term to describe the theory supporting a preference for Republican government had not yet been coined.

Consequently, when examining a sermon one should not fall into the trap of allowing every reference to a Whig, liberal, or republican idea serve as evidence that its writer was of a specific ideological or intellectual persuasion. To avoid this pitfall, one should use more sophisticated methods and look deeper. Neither can scholars count every sermonic reference to a thinker who has been classified as a liberal or a republican to mean that the clergy can be categorized as such. For instance, the ministers extensively referenced John Locke. This does not by itself mean that the clergy was composed of liberals. Lutz makes the important point that during the founding, Americans viewed Locke as a member of the commonwealthsmen and a contributor to the Whig theory of politics. Again, more evidence will be required in order to categorize the meaning of a reference.

The fourth category is "The Scottish Enlightenment." Lutz regards this as an important area of influence, particularly as a moral and economic philosophy, as well as a philosophy of history. Scottish Enlightenment theorists argued that the general economic welfare of society will best be promoted by allowing humans, who are by nature socially minded and benevolent, to pursue their own self-interest; the result being a material progress that will yield an ever increasing progress of liberty in history.

Lutz's fifth category is "The Enlightenment." Though it is a term the founding generation understood and employed, Lutz finds it problematic because under this banner many various, and often contradictory, ideas are lumped together. To clarify the category, he refines it to include four "enlightenments":

> a radical, antireligious strain that tended to emphasize pure reason; a natural-religion strain that attacked religious orthodoxy but was more interested in updating religion to be congruent with modern, empirical views of human nature than in rejecting religion; a moderate, liberal or constitutional strain that used both rationalism and empiricism and often emphasized the importance of economics; and a scientific or empirical strain that took advances in natural science as its model for advancing human knowledge about social, political, and economic matters.

The Enlightenment will be referenced frequently during this study. Where precision is required, these categories will be employed, but where precision is not needed, the term will be used in its more generic sense.

The final category is "Science and Politics." Lutz finds that much of the political writing of the era betrays the application of the assumptions of the newly emerging modern science to the study of politics. Lutz finds the writing is often based on the following three assumptions: "(1) There is an order in the universe, (2) we can know that order through the use of observation and reason, and (3) we can use that natural order in constructing our political institutions."[1]

By using these categories and definitions, the intellectual, ideological, and historical background of the clergy can be examined. Since the purpose of Part I is to provide a context for understanding the political

1. Lutz, *A Preface,* 114–34.

writings of Massachusetts Congregationalists from 1760 to 1790, it is important to note that it is merely a brief overview of Puritan and Congregationalist history and thought. To those well versed in this period, this summary will seem inadequate. Those looking for a deeper and more nuanced treatment of these issues and ideas should consult the footnotes and bibliography, which will acquaint the reader with scholarship that provides a far more in-depth understanding of this period. Examining the Puritan roots of Congregationalism, even in a summary fashion, is a thing worth doing, and it is to that end that Part I is dedicated.

1

THE NEW COVENANT
1627–1684

Thus stands the cause betweene God and us, wee are enetered into Covenant with him for this worke, wee have taken out a Commission, the Lord hath given us leave to draw our owne Articles wee have professed to enterprise these Accions upon these and these ends, wee have hereupon besought him of favour and blessing: Now if the Lord shall please to heare us, and bring us in peace to the place wee desire, then hath hee ratified this Covenant and sealed our Commission, [and] will expect a strickt performance of the Articles contained in it, but if wee shall neglect the observacion of these Articles which are the ends wee have propounded, and dissembling with our God, shall fall to embrace this present world and prosecute our carnall intencions, seekeing greate things for our selves and our posterity, the Lord will surely breake out in wrathe against us be revenged of such a perjured people and make us knowe the price of the breache of such a Covenant.

John Winthrop

John Winthrop laid out a vision that would captivate and inspire Puritans and Congregationalists for the next two centuries in his sermon "A Model of Christian Charity." Delivered aboard the *Arbella* before the Puritans landed in Massachusetts Bay, this was the sermon in which Winthrop interpreted for his compatriots the purpose of their expedition, and the conditions for success and failure.

> Now the onely way to avoyde this shipwracke and to provide for our posterity is to followe the Counsell of Micah, to doe Justly, to love mercy, to walke humbly with our God, for this end, wee must be knit together in this worke as one man, wee must entertaine each other in brotherly Affeccion, wee must be willing to abridge our selves of our superfluities, for the supply of others necessities, wee must uphold a familiar Commerce together in all meeknes, gentlenes, patience and liberallity, wee must delight in eache other, make others Condicions our owne rejoyce together, mourne together, labour, and suffer together, allwayes haveing before our eyes our Commission and Community in

the worke, our Community as members of the same body, soe shall wee keepe the unitie of the spirit in the bond of peace, the Lord will be our God and delight to dwell among us, as his owne people and will commaund a blessing upon us in all our wayes, soe that wee shall see much more of his wisdome power goodnes and truthe then formerly wee have been acquainted with, wee shall finde that the God of Israell is among us, when tenn of us shall be able to resist a thousand of our enemies, when hee shall make us a prayse and glory, that men shall say of succeeding plantacions: the lord make it like that of New England: for wee must Consider that wee shall be as a Citty upon a Hill, the eies of all people are uppon us; soe that if we shall deale falsely with our god in this worke wee have undertaken and soe cause him to withdrawe his present help from us, wee shall shame the faces of many of gods worthy servants, and cause theire prayers to be turned into Cursses upon us till wee be consumed out of the good land whether we are goeing: And to shutt upp this discourse with that exhortacion of Moses that faithfull servant of the Lord in his last farewell to Israell Deut. 30. Beloved there is now sett before us life, and good, deathe and evill in that wee are Commaunded this day to love the Lord our God, and to love one another to walke in his wayes and to keepe his Commaundments and his Ordinance, and his lawes, and the Articles of our Covenant with him that wee may live and be multiplyed, and that the Lord our God may blesse us in the land whether we goe to possesse it: But if our heartes shall turne away soe that wee will not obey, but shall be seduced and worshipp . . . other Gods our pleasures, and proffitts, and serve them; it is propounded unto us this day, wee shall surely perishe out of the good Land whether we passe over this vast Sea to possesse it.[1]

This covenant, along with its formula of blessings and curses, was reiterated in sermon after sermon throughout seventeenth- and eighteenth-century Massachusetts. While many modifications were made to the "Citty upon a Hill" during the next two centuries, the clergy remained committed to the covenant. This covenant constituted the fundamental source of identity and purpose of both Puritans and Congregationalists until well into the nineteenth century. So important is this covenant and its Puritan roots that Massachusetts Congregationalist political thought of the founding era cannot be understood without a full understanding of seventeenth-century Massachusetts Puritanism. The story of Massachusetts Puritanism, however, does not begin in America, but in England and Geneva.

---

1. John Winthrop, "Christian Charitie, A Modell Hereof." In *Puritan Political Ideas, 1558–1794,* ed. Edmund Morgan, 92–93.

Calvin, Geneva, and the Roots of Puritanism

The roots of the English Reformation can be traced to the three primary movements of the European Reformation: Lutheranism, Calvinism, and Anabaptism. According to Williston Walker, Lutheranism, though initially dominant in England, gave way to Calvinism in the mid-sixteenth century. Calvin's influence was transmitted to England directly through his letters and writings, and indirectly through the letters and writings of his "heralds," such as Martin Bucer and Heinrich Bullinger. Also, a number of Protestants exiled by Catholic Queen Mary (the Marian Exiles), including John Knox and Christopher Goodman, migrated to Geneva and were significantly influenced by Calvin during their stay. Taking advantage of the religious liberty the coronation of Queen Elizabeth signaled, they brought Calvinism with them when they returned to England.[2]

Calvinism's influence was perhaps most deeply felt through the Geneva Bible. Written in Geneva during the Marian Exile, the Geneva Bible contained a complete English translation of the Bible with notes that provided the reader with Calvinist commentary on the text. First printed in 1560, it quickly became the standard Puritan Bible and by the turn of the century was the most popular Bible in England. While eventually replaced in popularity by the King James Bible, it was the standard Bible of the Massachusetts Puritans throughout the seventeenth century. As a result, English Puritanism had a broad-based Calvinist foundation at the beginning of the seventeenth century.[3]

English Puritanism is a complex movement that is difficult to define. In his article "Defining Puritanism—Again?" Peter Lake lists three different definitions and offers a fourth. Stephen Foster describes still other ways to understand Puritanism and explains the difficulty faced in formulating a precise definition. Foster finds that at its heart Puritanism was "a movement: a loose and incomplete alliance of progressive Protestants, lay and clerical, aristocratic and humble" who were never quite sure of who

2. Williston Walker, *A History of the Congregational Churches in the United States,* 15; John T. McNeill, *The History and Character of Calvinism,* 309–14; and Michael Walzer, *The Revolution of the Saints: A Study in the Origin of Radical Politics,* 22–113.

3. Gerald T. Sheppard, "The Geneva Bible and English Commentary, 1600–1645," in *The Geneva Bible,* 1; Marvin W. Anderson, "The Geneva (Tomson/Junius) New Testament among Other English Bibles of the Period," in *The Geneva Bible,* 6; Christopher Hill, *The English Bible and the Seventeenth-Century Revolution,* 20.

they were.[4] Complicating matters, the word *Puritan* had several different meanings in the sixteenth and seventeenth centuries.

In the broadest sense of the term, *Puritan* refers to the members of the English Reformation who were dedicated to the full reform of the Church of England. The Puritans believed that Christianity constituted the foundation for the entirety of life. Puritans argued for the authority of the Bible not only in matters of personal morality and salvation but also in church administration, civil government, and social life. Since they were arguing for the complete and full "purification" of the church they were fitted with the name "Puritan."[5]

As the English Reformation developed, many disagreements emerged from within the movement. One concerned the proper relationship with the Church of England. Some argued that Puritanism should function as a reform movement within the church. Others argued that the church was hopelessly corrupt and lost, and that separation from the Anglicans and the establishment of a new church was the only option. Although the term *Puritan* can denote all reformation-minded English groups of this era, its primary usage came to denote only those reformers who remained within the Church of England. Those "Puritans" who advocated separation from the church came to be known as *Separatists*.

The two groups that initially formed Massachusetts, the Pilgrims and the Puritans, represent these two movements. The Pilgrims were a Separatist group that formed Plymouth Plantation; the Puritans, a non-Separatist group that formed Massachusetts Bay Colony.[6]

The Pilgrims and Plymouth Colony

The group that would become known as the Pilgrims was first formed by John Smyth in Gainsborough in 1602. By 1606, the Gainsborough church had grown into two Separatist congregations, one under the guidance of Smyth and the other shepherded by John Robinson. Both groups shared a conviction that the Church of England was irretrievably corrupt and lost, and since God called each individual to uncompromising obedience,

4. Peter Lake, "Defining Puritanism—Again?" in *Puritanism: Transatlantic Perspectives on a Seventeenth-Century Anglo-American Faith*, 3–29; Stephen Foster, *The Long Argument: English Puritanism and the Shaping of New England Culture, 1570–1700*, 5.
5. Perry Miller, *Errand into the Wilderness*, 15.
6. Richard E. Wentz, *Religion in the New World: The Shaping of Religious Traditions in the United States*, 68–69.

it would be sinful to not separate. This brought them and other Separatist groups into direct conflict with the Church of England and the English government, which was reluctant to grant toleration to Separatists. Due to increased government persecution, the two congregations immigrated to Holland, Smyth's in 1606 and Johnson's by 1608. They were tolerated in Holland, but life was difficult for the exiles; by 1620 they had made arrangements with the Virginia Company to emigrate to America on the *Mayflower.* After landing considerably north of the Virginia Company's holdings and being foiled in their attempts to sail south at the onset of winter, they created a settlement near Cape Cod and named it Plymouth.[7]

The principles used in establishing this new community were drawn from the teaching of Robert Browne, a sixteenth-century English Separatist whose thought was formative for both the Pilgrims and the Massachusetts Congregationalists. According to Browne,

> a Christian church is a body of professed believers in Christ, united to one another and to their Lord by a voluntary covenant. This covenant is the constitutive element which transforms an assembly of Christians into a Church. Its members are not all the baptized inhabitants of a kingdom, but only those possessed of Christian character. Such a church is under the immediate headship of Christ, and is to be ruled only by laws and officers of his appointment. To each church Christ has intrusted its own government, discipline, and choice of officers; and the abiding officers are those designated in the New Testament, the pastor, teacher, elders, deacons, and widows, whom the church is to select and set apart for various duties. But the presence of these officers does not relieve the ordinary member of responsibility for the welfare of the church to which he belongs. On the contrary, Christ is the immediate Lord not only of the church but of every member of it, and each member is responsible to him for the stewardship of the graces with which he has been intrusted.[8]

Browne's vision had important political implications; most notably, his church polity was extraordinarily democratic, and he advocated an unusually strict separation of church and state. Browne believed that "the civil authorities have no right to exercise lordship over spiritual concerns, or to enforce submission to any ecclesiastical system." Browne's framework was radically different from that which ruled England, but by

7. Walker, *A History*, 56–66; H. Roger King, *Cape Cod and Plymouth Colony in the Seventeenth Century*, 1–2.
8. Walker, *A History*, 38.

the spring of 1621 it formed the basis of the Pilgrim polity and would later influence Massachusetts Congregationalism.[9]

The Puritans and Massachusetts Bay Colony

The Puritans, though also critical of the Church of England, sought to reform it from within. They condemned Separatism as being biblically unjustified and were committed to remain in England to work for the reform of the Church of England. They believed that no human institution could ever be perfect, and as long as the church was not so corrupt that it could no longer be called a church, Christians were obligated to resist the temptation to separate and instead work for reform from within.[10]

Events in the early seventeenth century, however, made the Puritans reexamine this position. With the accession of Charles I and Archbishop Laud, the Church of England moved to a distinctly Catholic position, persecuting even non-Separatists. Moreover, when Charles I dismissed Parliament in 1629, it appeared to Puritans that the last bulwark against heresy and sin had crumbled. They did not want to separate, but feared for themselves, their children, and their nation.[11]

When a group of Puritans led by John White and John Endicott was presented with an opportunity to establish a community in Massachusetts, relocation seemed to hold hope as a solution to their dilemma. On March 4, 1629, this group was organized as the Massachusetts Bay Company. The charter of the Massachusetts Bay Company gave the company title to the land near the Charles River in Massachusetts Bay. Like other colonial charters, it established the sovereignty of the King and the Church of England and vested a board with governing powers. The charter, however, did not specify where the board should meet, and though London was the site undoubtedly intended, it was not so stipulated. This oversight created a loophole that, in the minds of the Puritans, turned the opportunity into a divinely engineered solution. An agreement was forged among the board members to convene the meetings in Massachusetts and make "the governor of the company . . . the governor of the colony, and the general court of the company . . . the legislative assembly of the colony."[12]

---

9. Ibid., 38–39; see also Henry Martyn Dexter, *The Congregationalism of the Last Three Hundred Years, as Seen in Its Literature . . .* , 61–128.

10. Edmund S. Morgan, *The Puritan Dilemma: The Story of John Winthrop*, 30–31, 40–44.

11. Walker, *A History*, 76–97.

12. Morgan, *Puritan Dilemma*, 46.

This permitted them an unprecedented amount of freedom to govern their own political and ecclesiastical affairs and at the same time allowed them to pledge loyalty to the English Crown and the Church of England. Seizing the chance, the company elected John Winthrop as governor, and he, along with hundreds of Puritans, immigrated to Massachusetts in 1629.

As Winthrop's sermon indicates, the Puritans believed that God had set them apart as a special people, with a special purpose, and had entered into a covenantal relationship with them. They believed God had given them an opportunity to realize their dream of creating a fully reformed community whose example could provide the impetus to complete the political and ecclesiastical reformation of England. If the citizens of Massachusetts would just obey the covenant, God would use their example and testimony to compel England and the rest of Europe to follow their example.[13]

Puritan Political Theology

With their mission so defined, the Puritans set out to fulfill it. Many obstacles, however, awaited them in Massachusetts Bay. Most pressing were problems of statecraft. Although the Puritans were politically inexperienced, they were equipped with a well-developed political theology.

The covenantal theology of the Calvinistic tradition provided the framework of their politics and worldview. Although *covenant* is a legal term found in the Old Testament, according to Meredith G. Kline, its meaning is rooted in the suzerain-vassal treaties of antiquity. "In these treaties an overlord addressed his vassals, sovereignly regulating their relations with him, with his other vassals, and with other nations."[14] As in the Bible, it was not a treaty between equal parties, but one between a king and his subjects, and it was a binding contract that stated each party's responsibilities and the punishment that would be meted if either side was delinquent.

According to the Puritans, the history of humanity is the history of covenants, from Adam to the present. In the first covenant, the *covenant of works,* Adam was given dominion over the earth with the stipulation that he execute his charge in accordance with God's intention for its use and development.

13. Ibid., 45–47.
14. Meredith G. Kline, *The Structure of Biblical Authority,* 27.

> God entered into such a bond with man as soon as He created him. He stipulated that if Adam performed certain things He would pledge Himself to reward Adam and Adam's posterity with eternal life. In order that man might know what was required of him, Adam was given specific injunctions in the form of the moral law. In addition, the law was implanted in his heart, built into his very being, so that he might perform his duties naturally and instinctively. The original covenant of works, therefore, is the law of nature, that which uncorrupted man would naturally know and by which he would naturally regulate his life.[15]

Adam was not only made aware of his duty but, as seen in Genesis 2:16–17, he was also made aware of the consequences for disobedience.

The covenant of works, however, was not just a covenant with Adam; it was also a covenant with humanity. Adam, who was created in the image of God, was given the opportunity and responsibility to decide the future of the human race. Had he lived obediently, immortality and a sinless nature would have been conferred upon humanity. Men and women would have lived eternally unimpinged by sin and death, and "no government would ever have been necessary among men; they would have done justice to each other without the supervision of a judge."[16] In choosing to sin, Adam corrupted his nature as well as the nature of his descendants. As Calvin says in his commentary on Romans,

> There are some interpreters who maintain that such was our ruin as a result of the sin of Adam, that we perished through no fault of our own, but merely because he had as it were sinned for us. Paul, however, expressly affirms that sin has spread to all who suffer the punishment of sin. He presses the point more closely when he shortly afterwards assigns a reason why all Adam's posterity are subject to the dominion of death. It is because we have all sinned. To sin, as the word is used here, is to be corrupt and vitiated. The natural depravity which we bring from our mother's womb, although it does not produce its fruits immediately, is still sin before God, and deserves His punishment. This is what is called original sin. As Adam at his first creation had received for his posterity as well as for himself the gifts of divine grace, so by falling from the Lord, in himself he corrupted, vitiated, depraved, and ruined our nature—having lost the image of God, the only seed which he could have produced was that which bore resemblance to himself. We have therefore all sinned, because we are

15. Miller, *Errand*, 61.
16. Ibid., 142.

all imbued with natural corruption, and for this reason are wicked and perverse.[17]

As a result of the Fall, the Puritans believed, the human heart is so corrupt that even though men can know God, they hate God and have no desire to conform themselves to his desires. As Romans 1 of the Geneva Bible states,

> For the wrath of God is reveiled from heaven against all ungodlinesse, and unrighteousnesse of men, which withhold the trueth in unrighteousness. For as much as that, which may be knownen of God, is manifest in them: for God hath shewed it unto them. For the invisible things of him, that is, his eternal power and Godhead are seene by the creation of the world, being considered in his works, to the intent that they should be without excuse: Because that when they knew God, they glorified him not as God, neither were thankfull, but became vaine in their thoughts, and their foolish heart was full of darkness. When they professed themselves to be wise they became fooles. For they turned the glory of the incorruptible God to the similitude of the image of a corruptible man, and of birds, and foure footed beasts, and of creeping things. Wherefore also God gave them up to their hearts lusts, unto uncleannes, to defile their owne bodies between themselves.[18]

Although the Puritans saw humanity as condemned by Adam's sin, they did not believe that death and destruction were immediate. Politics, established by fallen self-interested reason, creates enough order to temporarily counteract some of the chaos wrought by the Fall. While fallen reason is unable to save, it is able to see that an individual's interests are in some way related to the interests of others and the community. Consequently, rules for governing a post-Fall world can be established. For instance, the Puritans believed that in a post-Fall world a right to private property ought to exist.

> The Puritan theorists regarded property as antecedent to government, but not therefore noble. Children and the "just acquisitions" of man were . . . tied to carnality and passion. Given human nature, they could not be eliminated and were a necessary concession to man's lower nature. Government, however, as a later and higher form of human organization must regulate all of man's "propriety" for the public good.[19]

17. John Calvin, *The Epistles of Paul the Apostle to the Romans and to the Thessalonians*, 111–12.
18. *The Geneva Bible: The Annotated New Testament*, 1602 ed., Romans 1:18–24, 72.
19. McWilliams, *The Idea*, 127.

Although the Fall limited the amount of justice that can be established, the ability of humans to reason, albeit selfishly, made possible the existence of a "fallen" justice, which was able to provide humanity with enough order to survive.

Even though humans could use politics to delay annihilation, they could not avoid it. They stood under a death sentence from the Fall. God, however, forged new covenants designed for the redemption of the saints. The first of these covenants, the *covenant of redemption,* is an agreement between God the Father and God the Son. In it, "God covenanted with Christ that if he would pay the full price for the redemption of beleevers, they should be discharged. Christ hath paid the price, God must be unjust, or else hee must set thee free from all iniquitie."[20] With Christ satisfying the payment required by the covenant of redemption, salvation belongs to individuals who respond in faith, and for them the *covenant of grace* is established.

Men and women who respond to God's grace with faith in Christ receive the gift of salvation. Nothing besides faith is required. Nevertheless, according to the covenant of grace, a sign of election is an obedient life.

> In the covenant of grace, God, observing the form, contracts with man as with a peer. But since the Fall man is actually unable to fulfil the law or to *do* anything on his own initiative. Therefore God demands of him now not a deed but a belief, a simple faith in Christ the mediator. . . . But in this arrangement [the law] exists no longer as a command, the literal fulfillment of which is required of a man, but as a description of the goal of conduct toward which the saint incessantly strives. . . . [S]ince Christ has satisfied God by fulfilling the law, there is no necessity that we do it also. It is only necessary that we attempt it. God's agreement in the . . . covenant is that if a man will believe, he will receive the grace enabling him to approximate a holy life, but his failure to reach perfection will not be held against him.[21]

Because salvation is dependent on God's grace and not on human agency, no one can know with certainty the eternal disposition of their own soul or the souls of others. The covenant of grace implied, however, that indicators of a person's eternal destiny were a pious and virtuous lifestyle, along with the ability to speak of experiencing God's grace. The Puritans believed that such nonverbal and verbal testimony was an outward sign of the regenerative work of the Holy Spirit. So important were

---

20. Perry Miller, *The New England Mind: The Seventeenth Century,* 406.
21. Miller, *Errand,* 61–62, 82. See also Miller, *New England Mind: Seventeenth Century,* 365–97.

they that the Puritans made them the basis for both church membership and the political franchise.

Nevertheless, the Puritans realized that even these indicators were imperfect. Due to the dramatic effects of the Fall, sin would characterize the lives of even the saints. They saw that even after justification, men and women remain impotent to live righteously. The Fall so devastated the human heart that the mind, even the mind of the redeemed, was powerless to "will" a person into righteous behavior. As Paul says in Romans 7:14–24,

> For we know that the Law is spirituall, but I am carnal, sold under sinne. For I allow not that which I doe: for what I would, that I do not: but what i hate, that doe I. If I doe then that which I would not, I consent to the Law that it is good. Now then, it is not more I, that doe it, but sinne that dwelleth in me. For I know, that in me, that is, in my flesh dwelleth no good thing: for to wll ls present wlth mee: but I fìnd no meanes to performe that which is good: for i doe not the good thing, which I would, but the evill, which I would not, that I doe. Now if I doe that I would not, it is no more I that doe it, but the sinne that dwelleth in mee. I find then that when I would doe good, I am thus yoked, that evill is present with mee. For I delight in the Law of God concerning the inner man: But I see another Lawe in my members, rebelling against the Law of my minde, and leading me captive unto the Law of sinne, which is in my members. O wretched man that I am, who shal deliever me from this body of death![22]

It is important to note that this passage is descriptive of a regenerate man. According to the Puritans, the mind is capable of knowing the truth of God but is incapable of motivating righteous behavior. The mind is overruled by the soul's disposition to sin, a disposition that is never fully cured in this life. No man, regenerate or not, can do good by intellectual effort alone, hence the need for the covenant of grace. Any good that humans achieve is the consequence of the Holy Spirit overruling the impulses of their fallen nature. If humans are responsible for anything, it is the extent to which we open ourselves to God's work and allow the Holy Spirit to control our hearts and influence our minds.

Due to the pervasiveness of sin, God ordained two additional covenants to promote order and virtue in the human community: the *covenant of the church* and the *covenant of state*.[23] The covenant of the church was made between God and members of the visible church. In a distinction similar

22. *Geneva Bible,* 75.
23. McWilliams, *The Idea,* 125.

to that made by Augustine in *The City of God,* the Puritans distinguished between the "true saints," those God has redeemed, and the "visible saints, those who claim to be redeemed."[24] The true church will emerge only when Christ forms it at the end of history. Until then God has established a covenant with the visible church, those men and women who claim dedication to Christ and his Kingdom. The visible church is a community of people dedicated to facilitating the worship of God and encouraging its members to live piously and virtuously. It is a voluntary community ruled by a covenant. Perry Miller describes it:

> The saints come together and formally agree to carry out in ecclesiasti-
> cal life the obligations to which they stand individually bound by their
> covenant with God. The duties and requirements are those determined
> in the covenant of grace. The church compact is the agreement of the
> people in a body to constitute an institution which will facilitate the
> achievement of these ends.[25]

All members of the community were required to attend the parish church, but participation in the governing of the church was limited to male property owners who affirmed Puritan doctrine, led pious and virtuous lives, and could testify to a personal experience of God's redeeming grace in their life. The importance of this spiritual experience cannot be underestimated. The Puritans placed great value on spirituality. Although they were a community that stressed virtuous and moral living, conversion required a lifelong spiritual pilgrimage. Consequently, spirituality was the focus of their ecclesiastical life. Morality and virtue were important but secondary. Church membership was withheld from those unable to testify to spiritual rebirth.[26]

The Congregational polity was democratic, with each member given one vote. According to John T. McNeill, the Puritans were undecided about church polity, and when they first arrived they were considering the Presbyterian option. That they chose Congregationalism may be due to a visit from a member of the Pilgrim community, Dr. Samuel Fuller, in May 1629. In any event, when the Puritans established their first church

24. Herbert Deane, *The Political and Social Ideas of St. Augustine*, 24.

25. Miller, *Errand*, 91.

26. Edmund S. Morgan, *Visible Saints: The History of a Puritan Idea*, 88–112; Edmund S. Morgan, *The Puritan Family: Religion and Domestic Relations in Seventeenth-Century New England*, 134–40; T. H. Breen, *The Character of the Good Ruler: A Study of Puritan Political Ideas in New England, 1630–1730*, 49; and Charles E. Hambrick-Stowe, *The Practice of Piety: Puritan Devotional Disciplines in Seventeenth-Century New England*.

in Salem, they did so according to Congregational principles, and Puritan Congregationalism was informally born. Representatives of the Plymouth Church attended the founding of the Salem Church to extend "the right hand of fellowship," and throughout the century the Plymouth Church participated fully with the other "Puritan" churches as members of a common Congregationalist polity. The Pilgrims and Puritans unofficially constituted a common Congregationalist denomination throughout the seventeenth century but were not legally joined until England gave Massachusetts jurisdiction over Plymouth in the Charter of 1691.[27]

In addition to church covenants, the Puritans also believed God regulated post-Fall human affairs through his covenants with nations. As we have seen, the Puritans believed that all humans, through the light of reason, are aware of God's design for social life, but because of selfishness they cannot fully comply with it. If left to their own desires and if in possession of the necessary power, they will want to subvert the social order for their own ends. No one, however, is powerful enough to realize this dream, and most humans are aware of it. Consequently, God ordains that human self-interest pushes humans to form nations to protect themselves from others with evil intent. Although the best government they can establish is imperfect, it is preferable to chaos. Moreover, God covenants with each nation to reward those that succeed and punish those that fail. To those nations who obey God's laws, he "promised prosperity and happiness in this world. . . . They [are], of course, incapable of perfect obedience. . . . But it was possible to maintain at least outward obedience, and God would prosper the community that showed Him this degree of honor in its actions."[28]

The nations that violate the covenant of state are destroyed directly by the hand of God or indirectly through the consequences of their sin. The covenant of state establishes politics as a mechanism to promote justice in a sinful human community. Government is essential even in communities where the visible saints dominate because of the inherent weakness of the regenerated will. Even the visible saints require a government to help them fulfill the covenant of state.

As to the recommended form of government, the Puritans were theoretically noncommittal. They taught that Scripture mandated no ideal form of government. As evidence for this, they pointed to the different

27. McNeill, *The History*, 338; Walker, *A History*, 100–101; Wentz, *Religion*, 70–71; and Dexter, *Congregationalism*, 416–18, 437, 464.
28. Morgan, *Puritan Political Ideas*, xxi.

forms allowed by God in the Old Testament and the lack of normative statements concerning governmental form in both Testaments. The Puritans believed that God gave nations constitutional latitude. Government originates in the consent of the people, and citizens are free to construct their own governments, choose their own rulers, and make their own laws.

In reality, however, the Puritans preferred a republican form of government, such as the one Israel employed during the period of Judges. They believed that republican government was least prone to corruption and most likely to encourage righteousness, and they established one soon after arrival.[29]

Doing so was an act of political cunning. The charter established a very undemocratic system. The colony was to be governed by a board. The board's members, "known as 'freemen,' were to meet four times a year in a 'Great and General Court,' to make laws for both company and colony. Once a year, at one of these courts, they would elect a governor, a deputy governor, and eighteen 'assistants' for the coming year, to manage affairs between meetings of the General Court." At one of the first meetings of the General Court, Governor Winthrop designated all church members as "freemen." This decision established republican government in Massachusetts. The freemen selected the assistants who "were transformed from an executive council into a legislative assembly." This assembly was given authority to select the governor and his cabinet. In this way the charter became the first Massachusetts Constitution.[30]

It is important to note that less than one-fifth of the inhabitants of Massachusetts were freemen or citizens. Nevertheless, even though the others were disenfranchised, they "had equality before the law, property rights, police protection; they were taxed no more than the citizens or submitted to no indignities, but they were allowed no voice in the government or in choice of ministers, and only by the mere force of numbers gained any influence in town meetings."[31]

Although the Puritans were supportive of republican government, they were no friend of democracy. Though all public offices were filled annually through elections, the Puritans did not embrace an unlimited notion of popular sovereignty. Rulers "received their authority from God, not from the people, and were accountable to God, not to the

---

29. Breen, *The Character,* 48; Miller, *Errand,* 147.
30. Morgan, *Puritan Dilemma,* 85–91.
31. Miller, *Errand,* 150.

people."³² The Puritan concept of *calling* maintained that God calls certain individuals to government ministry. The job of the electorate is to determine who God is calling and, having done that, to leave governing to the magistrates. For the Puritans, "a proper government was one in which a limited number of men, whether one, few, or many, exercised authority over the rest of society. They might be hereditary or elective, but once placed in the office to which God, by whatever means, had called them, it was up to them to do the governing.³³ Although the ruler was accountable to God, there were prescribed limits to his power. "The power of the ruler should be exercised in accordance with established fundamental law."³⁴ Consequently, the people were entitled to hold their rulers accountable to God's legal standards, and the rulers were obliged to return the favor.

There was no concept of unlimited or absolute rights of citizens at this time. Citizens were protected because government is bound to fundamental law, but "by entering . . . the covenant with each other, the citizens renounce all natural liberty, surrender the right to seek for anything that they might lust after, and retain only the freedom that 'is maintained and exercised in a way of subjection to authority.' "³⁵ Citizens and magistrates together bear the responsibility for keeping the covenant. If government is unjust or if citizens live unrighteously, the entire nation is punished. Hence, magistrates of exceptional ability and character are essential to keeping the terms of the covenant of state.

These two covenants, the covenants of church and state, form the foundation of the Puritan understanding of religion and politics. The Puritans were careful to maintain the separation of the institutions of church and state, with each having different responsibilities. Officials from each realm were barred from holding office in the other. The responsibility of the church was to promote the spiritual purity of its members and to be obedient to the mission of the church as articulated in Scripture. On the one hand, the church was called to preach the word to all people, even though it had jurisdiction over only its own members. On the other hand, the state was responsible to promote outward obedience of all citizens to biblical standards of justice. "The state . . . representing God's kingly authority, was very much a thing of this world. Its business was to enforce His laws on men whose wills were corrupted by the fall of

32. Morgan, *Puritan Dilemma*, 94.
33. Morgan, *Puritan Political Ideas*, xviii.
34. Miller, *Errand*, 146.
35. Ibid., 149.

Adam. Its methods were not spiritual but temporal: the whip, the prison, the gallows, armies, navies, sheriffs, constables, judges. The state, like the church, was a work of God."[36]

Although the church and state were separate, religion and politics were not. The special covenant God made with Massachusetts insured that they would be deeply linked. The Puritans envisioned church and state as working together to keep their covenantal obligation to maintain a virtuous and pious community. Church and state must be linked to promote this end.

> Church and state were intimately linked in Puritan theory because they were part of a single endeavor to produce the best life available to men. A "separation" of the two presupposes not only a church unconcerned with this life—a manifest absurdity, since its members are living men—but that a state can be complete if it is concerned only with worldly things. Given the Puritan view of human nature, that concept was no less absurd. . . . The purely secular state, Baxter wrote, is to the true commonwealth as "an idiot is to a reasonable man" lacking a true understanding of man's nature and his perennial discontent with the world and worldly things, such a state cannot treat him with justice.[37]

The Puritan clergy envisioned life as a pilgrimage. "Life lived in the Spirit was set against life in the world of sin." The avoidance of sin was an important part of the successful pilgrimage; an obedient church and a godly state could be a tremendous help to the pilgrim.[38] The state, though institutionally separate from the church, had the mission of supporting the work of the church and aiding the pilgrim by whatever means possible. Enforcing God's law and encouraging virtue and piety were the most important aspects of that mission.

The following excerpt from the Cambridge Platform of 1648 demonstrates the extent to which the church and state worked together to promote righteousness.

> 2 Church-government stands in no opposition to civil government of comon-welths, nor any intrencheth upon the authority of Civil Magistrates in their jurisdictions; nor any whit weakneth their hands in governing; but rather stregthneth them, & furthereth the people in yielding more hearty & conscionable obedience uto them. . . .
>
> The powr & authority of Magistrates is not for the restraining of churches, or any other good workes, but for helping in & furthering therof. . . .

36. Morgan, *Puritan Political Ideas,* xxvii.
37. McWilliams, *The Idea,* 125.
38. Hambrick-Stowe, *Practice of Piety,* 278.

4 It is not in the powr of Magistrates to compell their subjects to become church-members, & to partake at the Lords table. . . .

5 As it is unlawfull for church-officers to meddle with the sword of the Magistrate, so it is ulawful for the Magistrate to meddle with the work proper to church-officers. . . .

6 It is the duty of the Magistrate, to take care of matters of religion, & to improve his civil authority for the observing of the duties commanded in the first, as well as for observing of the duties commanded in the second table. . . .

7 The object of the power of the Magistrate, are not things meerly inward, & so not subject to his cognisance & view, as unbeleife hardness of heart, erronious opinions not vented; but only such things as are acted by the outward man; neither is their powr to be exercised, in commanding such acts of the outward man, & punishing the neglect therof, as are but meer invetions, & devices of men; but about such acts, as are commanded & forbidden in the word; yea such as the word doth clearly determine, . . . In these times he of right ought to putt forth his authority, though oft-times actually he doth it not.

8 Idolatry, Blasphemy, Heresy, venting corrupt & pernicious opinions, that destroy the foundation, open contempt of the word preached, prophanation of the Lords day, disturbing the peacable administration & exercise of the worship & holy things of God, & the like, are to be restrayned, & punished by the civil authority. If any church one or more shall grow schismaticall, rending it self from the communion of other churches, or shall walke incorrigibly or obstinately in any corrupt way of their own, contrary to the rule of the word; in such case the Magistrate is to put forth his coercive powr, as the matter shall require.[39]

As the platform depicts, the state played a central role in Puritan life. While it may appear the importance of religion makes the church superior to the state, it was the state that had ascendancy. As point 8 makes clear, the Puritans gave the state the power to define true religion, enforce purity of religion, and determine limits of toleration.

The power of the state vis-à-vis the church raised a crucial problem for the Puritans. How were they to keep the state pure? In Massachusetts the clergy was given an advisory role in politics but not allowed to hold public office. To ensure the input of the visible saints, the Puritans allowed only male church members with property to vote and hold office. Linking the franchise with church membership enabled the church to retain an indirect influence in politics and as a safeguard in helping Massachusetts resist secularization.

The issue of tolerance was problematic for the Puritans. While deterring vice always challenged the government, the real challenge lay

39. Williston Walker, *The Creeds and Platforms of Congregationalism*, 235–37.

in defining the limits of orthodoxy and determining what to do with those who crossed the line. One of the Puritans' primary motivations to immigrate was the need for religious freedom, but for the Puritans, religious freedom did not include toleration.[40]

> There was, it is true, a strong element of individualism in the Puritan creed; every man had to work out his own salvation, each soul had to face his maker alone. But at the same time, the Puritan philosophy demanded that in society all men . . . be marshaled into one united array. The lone horseman, the single trapper, the solitary hunter was not a figure of the Puritan frontier; Puritans moved in groups and towns, settled in whole communities, and maintained firm government over all units. . . . The government of Massachusetts, and of Connecticut as well, was a dictatorship, . . . not of a single tyrant, or of an economic class, or of a political faction, but of the holy and regenerate. Those who did not hold with the ideals entertained by the righteous, or who believed God had preached other principles, or who desired that in religious belief, morality, and ecclesiastical preferences all men should be left at liberty to do as they wished—such persons had every liberty, as Nathaniel Ward said, to stay away from New England. If they did come, they were expected to keep their opinions to themselves; if they discussed them in public or attempted to act upon them, they were exiled; if they persisted in returning, they were cast out again; if they still came back, as did four Quakers, they were hanged on Boston Common. And from the Puritan point of view, it was good riddance.[41]

Maintaining that intolerance is a prerequisite for religious liberty seems inconsistent to the modern mind, but to the Puritans this was not so. The Puritans' concept of liberty is the most important element in their political thought. It was for liberty that they left their homes and came to Massachusetts Bay, and no sacrifice was too great to stay free. What they understood by *liberty*, however, is profoundly different from the modern concept and different from the understanding of Congregationalists of the revolutionary period.

John Winthrop articulated the Puritan view in a speech given on liberty in 1645.

> Winthrop argues that individuals, in a natural state, before grace has been given them, are at absolute liberty to do anything they can, to lie, steal, murder; obviously he is certain that natural men, being what they are, will do exactly these things unless prevented. But when men become regenerate they are then at "liberty" to do only what God

40. Miller, *Errand,* 141–52.
41. Ibid., 143–44.

commands. And God commands certain things for the group as a whole as well as for each individual. Regenerate men, therefore, by the very fact of being regenerate, come together, form churches and a state upon explicit agreements, in which they all promise to live with one another according to the laws and for the purposes of God.[42]

According to the Puritans, humans are free to make whatever laws they desire, even those that violate the covenant of nature and natural law. Such covenants and laws are unstable, inadequate, unworkable, and ultimately result in a personal and/or corporate chaos in which bondage, and not liberty, triumphs. God allows human beings to make decisions that result in loss of liberty. The regenerate, however, are not to exercise freedom in such an unwise manner. Rather, they are to use their freedom to make choices that allow them to live free of spiritual and social bondage. This requires them to use their freedom to do that "which is good, just, and honest."[43] To the Puritan mind, toleration is at odds with liberty and will ultimately undermine its enjoyment.

To realize the blessings of the liberty that would come by keeping the covenant, the Puritans designed a constitution in which adherence to God's covenants was codified and enforced by magistrates selected by the visible church. Their political loyalty lay with England, but their covenantal hope lay in this constitution's someday forming the foundation of a new England and a new Europe.

Puritan preaching reflected the importance and burden of the covenant. The ministers frequently referred to their society as the new Israel, with New England being the Promised Land. Just as God had guided human history to give Israel an opportunity to be the agent of redemption for the world, so they perceived that God had been working in human history since the resurrection of Christ to give them this opportunity. A. W. Plumstead summarizes their self-understanding:

> The Second Adam, Christ, reaffirmed God's covenant with man, and the early little pockets of Christian churches after his death were as close to the ideal communities of God as history had, until 1630, shown. But it would seem impossible to preserve such purity for long; soon the church fell into decay, and entered upon a long sleep in the dark ages of Roman domination. Then the spirit of purification rose up out of its sleep in a baptism of fire; the Protestant revolution began a new chapter in the quest for God's covenanted society, and Cartwright and

42. Ibid., 148–49.
43. Ibid., 149.

Ames in England carried the work of Luther and Calvin to theoretical perfection. England reformed, but failed to progress beyond a slightly improved church. At this point, when the energy and learning needed to create the long awaited society were never more available, geography played its part. America was discovered.[44]

Already possessing high standards, the Puritans magnified the importance of their experiment by identifying themselves as the new Israel. Were they to fail, they would fail not only themselves and their descendants, but, as they saw it, the entire world and posterity. Understandably, the great fear of ministers was that New England would not uphold the covenant, not realize its promise, and would suffer the judgment and fate of the first Israel. The task of constructing "A Citty upon a Hill" consumed them.

From Vision to Reality

Having explicated their worldview, we can now turn our attention to its application. Perry Miller may have summed it up best when he said, "As this theory stands on paper, it is, like so many edifices of the Puritan mind, almost perfect. When it was realized in practice, however, there were . . . difficulties that soon became apparent."[45]

The first generation of immigrants encountered a number of difficulties. They had to endure the physical, emotional, and spiritual hardships of building a colony. Many colonists died of sickness and disease. But even more difficult were the theological disagreements that threatened to divide them. Perhaps the biggest challenge the first generation confronted concerned separatism. Establishing boundaries appropriate for a godly community proved contentious, as the banishment of Anne Hutchinson and Roger Williams demonstrated. It was hoped that the adoption of the Cambridge Platform in 1648 would stabilize the colony and allow it to realize its promise.[46]

Such hope proved ill founded. Ultimately, the Puritan community was based not on moral rules, but on a spiritual life that had moral implications. Given sin, government would always be needed to punish and deter sin. The community's hope lay not in government, but in the spiritual regeneration of its citizens. Without this spiritual basis, the

44. A. W. Plumstead, ed., *The Wall and the Garden,* 26.
45. Miller, *Errand,* 150.
46. Morgan, *Puritan Dilemma.*

community was not viable. Government was important, but spirituality was the foundation of the community. To ensure the spiritual health of the community, the franchise was extended only to church members. This provision worked well for first-generation immigrants since many, if not most, professed Christianity before coming to Massachusetts. The problem came as the second generation "showed some decline from the ardent type of piety which marked many of the founders."[47] The religious experience and conviction that the Puritans valued so highly were lacking in the lives of their children. A question arose concerning what to do with those members of the second generation who had been admitted to the church as children but who had not experienced Christian conversion. Apart from its theological importance, the debate had political importance: Should the franchise be extended beyond the "visible saints"? Due to the decline in piety, a shrinking percentage of the population enjoyed the franchise, and questions concerning the political legitimacy of the regime were heard with greater frequency. The debate raged for some time and was resolved by the *halfway covenant,* which created another class of church membership. These children were allowed to be baptized but denied communion as well as the ecclesiastical or political franchise.

This decision illustrates the ongoing importance the Puritans attached to spirituality. Even though they modified the Cambridge Platform, they did not compromise on political spirituality. Only the visible saints would continue to rule. The halfway covenant, however, did not arrest the fall of piety. As the seventeenth century progressed, the Puritans were presented with an ever more perplexing problem. Even though political participation was denied the unbelievers, their immorality threatened to breach the founding covenant. Neither the magistrates nor the ministers knew quite what to do. The moral and spiritual condition of Massachusetts looked so desperate that in 1679 a synod was called in Boston to address the problem. The report they issued, *The Necessity of Reformation,* reflected their perception of the situation. It set forth the

> Synod's sense of the decay of godliness in the land; of the increase of pride; neglect of worship; sabbath breaking; lack of family government; censurings, intemperance, falsehood, and love of the world: and recommending, as means for combating these evils, insistence on strictness in admission to communion; the strengthening of family and

47. Walker, *A History,* 171.

> church discipline; the appointment of a pastor, teacher, and ruling
> elder in each church . . . the payment of adequate ministerial salaries;
> the careful execution of law, especially of the statutes regulating the
> sale of spirits; a renewal of church covenants; and care for schools,
> especially for Harvard College.[48]

Given the moral condition of the colony, the ministers were amazed that
God "hath waited and spared so long such an unworthy people."[49]

Dealing with immorality, however, was not easy. Enforcing moral codes
required a political fortitude that neither community nor magistrates
long retained, particularly as the seventeenth century progressed. The
clergy frequently appealed to the magistrates to enforce the moral code,
but finding it difficult to deal with widespread vice, the magistrates
became increasingly reluctant to do so. Instead, the magistrates called on
the ministers to do better at promoting Christianity among the general
population in the belief that a spiritual revival would more effectively
reform the colony. Neither side was successful, and each blamed the
other for their lack of success.[50]

The ministers came to see themselves as the Jeremiahs of Massachusetts, exhorting people to repent and pleading with the government to
enforce the moral codes lest God should punish the colony and termi-
nate this divine experiment. They did it with such regularity that they
developed a style of preaching called the *jeremiad*. A typical jeremiad was
a sermon in which the minister would reexamine God's covenant with the
Puritans, review the rewards for obedience and the punishments for disobedience, survey God's miraculous work in the history of Massachusetts,
and, like Jeremiah, lament the present sinful condition of the colony and
its people, concluding with a call for repentance.[51]

The increased use of the jeremiad following the Boston synod draws
attention to the difficulties the Puritans had in realizing the vision of the
founders. Other challenges faced the colony at this time, including royal
interference via the Navigation Acts of 1660 and 1663, and King Philip's
War.[52] Nevertheless, the Puritans persevered in their mission until 1684,
when their charter was abruptly revoked. This move threatened the entire
experiment and significantly altered the future of the colony.

48. Walker, *A History*, 187.
49. Stout, *New England Soul*, 105.
50. Breen, *The Character*, 87–133.
51. Sacvan Bercovitch, *The American Jeremiad*.
52. Breen, *The Character*, 87–133; and Michael J. Puglisi, *Puritans Besieged: The
Legacies of King Philip's War in the Massachusetts Bay Colony*.

2

THE SECOND CHARTER
AND THE DAWN OF CONGREGATIONALISM
1684–1760

It has often been said that the end of the seventeenth and the beginning of the eighteenth century mark the first real break with the Middle Ages in the history of European thought. Even though the Renaissance and Reformation transformed many aspects of the Western intellect, still it was not until the time of Newton that the modern scientific era began; only then could men commence to regard life in this world as something more than preparation for life beyond the grave.

Perry Miller

The Puritan experiment ended on October 23, 1684. Disgusted with the lack of control and colonial disobedience, the government of King Charles II recommended, and the English Court of Chancery approved, the cancellation of the original charter of the Massachusetts Bay Company. Massachusetts politics was in turmoil until one of the most respected Puritan ministers, Increase Mather, returned from England with a new charter in 1691. Although Increase Mather did his best to downplay the changes introduced by the new document, it represented a new direction in politics. The Puritan era was over; the Congregationalist era had begun.

The Glorious Revolution, the Second Charter, and the Demise of the Puritan Constitution: 1684–1691

The English government had been concerned about Massachusetts politics since the colony's inception. The Puritans, taking advantage of a loophole in the Massachusetts charter, had removed the seat of government to Massachusetts and began asserting that under the terms of the charter acts of the Crown "had no force in Massachusetts until confirmed by its own authority."[1] This effectively removed control of the colony

---

1. David S. Lovejoy, *The Glorious Revolution in America,* 132.

from the Crown to the colonists, allowing them more independence than had been intended and more than any other colony possessed. Although Massachusetts was officially bound to the king, Parliament, and the Church of England, the Puritans came to adopt practices contrary to those allowed in England. To make matters worse, the colony regularly disregarded directives from the English government. For instance, Massachusetts ignored the Navigation Acts by trading directly with foreign nations, thus denying revenue to England.

The colony's critics made the English government aware of these violations, but because the government had more pressing matters, Massachusetts was largely left alone. Under Charles II, however, matters changed, and in October 1684 the English Court of Chancery found the colony disobedient and cancelled the charter. "By that act every corporation created, every town government established, every sale of land effected by virtue of powers conferred by the Charter of 1629, was made void. The whole legal establishment of the churches, the entire body of colonial law, was swept away."[2] The Puritan constitution had been nullified.

Because of the death of Charles II, a new government was not set up until May 1686, but it was profoundly different:

> The new administrative system, called the Dominion of New England, consolidated the colonies of Connecticut, Massachusetts, Rhode Island, Plymouth, and New Hampshire. Later New York and New Jersey were added, and the entire territory was placed under the control of a single royal governor. This official, acting with the members of an appointed council, held complete executive and legislative . . . jurisdiction. The Lords of Trade set several general guidelines for the new government to follow. First, ignoring local practices, the imperial planners made no provision for the continuation of elective or representative assemblies. All Dominion rulers were to be appointed either by the king or by the governor. Second, the Lords announced that the new government would guarantee freedom of worship. . . . And last, the planners instructed Dominion rulers to issue land grants in the king's name and to collect a small quitrent upon all acreage in the territory.[3]

This represented a radical restructuring of the New England political system, especially that of Massachusetts. Although restructuring was painful to the inhabitants, it was short-lived. When the colonists learned of the

---

2. Walker, *A History,* 192.
3. Breen, *The Character,* 138.

overthrow of Charles's successor, James II, and the establishment of William and Mary on the throne during the Glorious Revolution, New Englanders effected their own revolution by deposing Edmund Andros, the dominion governor.

The overthrow of Andros brought about a constitutional crisis. Because of the turmoil in England, no new charter was immediately forthcoming, and the citizens were left to form a provisional government. One might naturally expect them to reinstate the first charter, but they did not. Rather, they decided "to reestablish a representative government modeled on the old charter with the significant difference that all landowners and taxpayers could now vote in provincial elections regardless of church membership status."[4] By removing the religious and spiritual basis of the franchise, the leaders of Massachusetts effectively ended the Puritan regime.

That a profound change had occurred in Massachusetts political thought can be seen in the rhetoric and discourse of the interim period. From 1689 to 1691 the pamphleteers who sought to justify the provisional system did so using language and ideas that differed profoundly from those of their Puritan fathers. As T. H. Breen recounts:

> The revolutionary authors of 1689 insisted that a good ruler had to defend popular rights, especially those associated with private property. The rebels claimed that they had acted upon the dictates of conscience when they locked Andros in jail; but conscience spoke a different language in this period than it had in Winthrop's generation. Religious considerations alone no longer seemed capable of stirring men to civil disobedience; and, according to the New England writers, Andros was unacceptable, chiefly because he had seized their personal holdings through illegal and arbitrary procedures. In the early decades of the Puritan commonwealth the foundation of civil power had been godliness, and Puritan freemen made certain that "visible saints" controlled the town as well as the colonial government. But, by the time of the Glorious Revolution, property—more than godliness—served as the basis for political leadership and participation. . . .
>
> For the most part, they dropped the scriptural rhetoric which had permeated much of the political writing in the old charter period, and attacked Andros's government for defects which had little or nothing to do with Puritanism. . . . What the Puritan pamphleteers were doing in effect was to transform the Moseses and Nehemiahs of former generations into guardians of property.[5]

4. Stout, *New England Soul,* 115.
5. Breen, *The Character,* 136–37, 152–53.

Massachusetts had changed, and so had the clergy. Given the ministers' commitment to the covenant, as well as their historic commitment to the Puritan constitution, a clerical outcry over the changes would be expected, yet little came. In fact, the clergy played a pivotal role in making the changes permanent.

Although the citizens of Massachusetts appreciated the freedom they secured following the Glorious Revolution, they were anxious for these freedoms to be codified in a new charter as soon as possible. Increase Mather was sent to London as the colony's chief negotiator. When the new charter was issued, the colony's first response was disappointment. The colonists had hoped to see their earlier autonomy fully reinstated, but with William wanting to administer the colony more closely, this did not happen.

> This charter . . . reserved to the king the appointment of the highest offices of government, and a right to reject obnoxious laws. It swept away all ecclesiastical tests for the franchise, even such indirect and partial tests as had continued since 1664; it granted freedom of worship to Protestants of all shades. But it left to Massachusetts a legislature of which the Lower House was directly chosen by the people, and in which the Upper House was still measurably under the control of the popular representatives,—a legislature too, which held the purse, and hence had a potent means of control over all branches of the government. The old local governments of the towns were left undisturbed; and this, with the power of taxation which was in the hands of the legislature, insured the ascendancy of [Congregationalism].[6]

The citizens, the clergy, and the elected officials of Massachusetts objected strenuously to the loss of political autonomy, especially to the fact that the governor would be chosen by the Crown. Yet their objections were dismissed and the new charter implemented.

The new charter also made official the new relationship that had emerged between church and state since the Glorious Revolution.

> First, enforced toleration meant that it no longer mattered whether or not orthodox Congregationalists governed Massachusetts. The ruler's main functions: protecting property, keeping the peace, and waging war, could be performed equally well by persons from any Protestant denomination. . . . Second, toleration forced the Congregational leaders to stand on their own; for after 1691 ministers could no longer expect any assistance from civil government.[7]

6. Walker, *A History,* 196.
7. Breen, *The Character,* 199.

What is most surprising about the public reactions to the new charter is the paucity of clergy opposition. The new charter undermined key aspects of the Puritans' worldview and their political power, yet significant clergy opposition was never mounted. Increase Mather and his son, Cotton, also a minister, convinced other clergy as well as many leading citizens to accept the terms of the new charter. While there was some dissent, the clergy provided some of the most ardent support for this change, and the colony accepted the new terms with relatively little protest.[8]

A number of factors contributed to their success in convincing fellow clergymen. First, the Mathers argued that the new charter was a more effective means to fulfill God's covenant with Massachusetts. Throughout this era, Massachusetts continued to see itself as the "Citty upon a Hill," with the covenant continuing to form the foundation of its political life.

Without doubt, the decline in piety and virtue had placed the Puritan constitution in a difficult position during its final decade. The poor spiritual condition of the colony made government enforcement of moral and theological orthodoxy increasingly difficult, especially after the hanging of the Quakers on Boston Common.[9] The second charter approached these problems in a new way, and the ministers were willing to experiment. Whereas the previous constitution was anchored in the spirituality of the visible saints, the second charter focused on ethical behavior. No longer was spirituality a *political* requirement. The new constitution regarded religion as important but not as a criterion for citizenship. The Congregationalists allowed the further separation of church and state in the hope that a superior way had been discovered to manage the complex relationship between religion and politics.

The second charter replaced political spirituality with ethics and religious freedom. Its defenders hoped that Christianity and virtue would better flourish in this new environment. The Congregationalists still believed that only Christianity could produce a virtuous people. They just believed that this new relationship between church and state would better promote Christianity and virtue. While it may appear that the new charter devalued religion, its defenders disagreed. They had merely adopted a new tactic in their quest to create the virtuous citizens needed to keep the covenant. As far as they were concerned, Christianity was still the foundation on which any adequate political charter must rest.

8. Ibid., 181–202 passim.
9. Ibid.

This is the second reason for the Mathers' success in persuading the ministers: they were able to convince the clergy that, despite the movement toward toleration, the charter continued to be based on Christianity, and that for all practical purposes nothing had changed; the Congregational Church retained its hegemony. The charter mandated Protestant toleration but did not disestablish the Congregational Church. Increase Mather had negotiated the charter in such a way that "the old local governments of the towns were left undisturbed; and this, with the power of taxation which was in the hands of the legislature, insured the ascendancy of the form of ecclesiastical polity which had heretofore been dominant in New England."[10] The church had long benefited from its position as the established church of a parish system, and this system was allowed to continue. The parish system, which originated in Europe, divided Massachusetts geographically "for purposes of worship, instruction, and discipline."[11] Everyone within the boundary of the parish was under the jurisdiction of the church and bound to give financial support through taxes. Although all of the parish's legal voters had a right to participate in the calling of its minister, the clear majority of voters in each parish were Congregationalist, minimizing the political impact of this provision into the nineteenth century.[12]

The real benefit of the parish system to the Congregational Church was not the financial support but the recognition of the Congregational Church as the center of community life in each parish. The meetinghouse frequently functioned as the town hall, and the church service was not only the key weekly spiritual event but also the primary social event.

> Recent estimates suggest that a majority of adults in the eighteenth-century colonies were regular church attenders. Though the worship of God was no doubt the primary motive for church going, . . . church attendance served a number of non-spiritual needs. . . . Churches in both country and town were vital centers of community life, as government proclamations were broadcast from the pulpit and news of prices and politics was exchanged in the churchyard. In a society formed by the uprooted communities of the Old World, . . . the church congregation served as a primary agency behind which immigrants received something of what they left behind.[13]

10. Walker, *A History,* 196.
11. Winthrop S. Hudson, *Religion in America,* 14–15.
12. Walker, *A History,* 220–21.
13. Patricia U. Bonomi, *Under the Cope of Heaven: Religion, Society and Politics in Colonial America,* 87–88.

Because Congregationalism retained its political dominance, ministers could easily accept the Mathers' argument that nothing important had changed. This led many members of the clergy to conclude that "the original supposition that a theocratic state was essential to covenant keeping was wrong. . . . If pure worship and voluntary submission to God's Word were achieved through the new charter . . . then the theocratic state could disappear without detriment to the federal covenant."[14]

Although not obvious at the time, something important had changed. Under the new charter it was now more important than ever that the church work to create citizens that would demand government honor the economic and political agenda of Congregationalism. Under the first charter the parish was given authority to make all religious decisions for citizens within its boundaries. With only one church per parish, the Congregational Church was dominant. The Charter of 1691, however, allowed other churches to form within parish boundaries. Tax money previously reserved for the Congregational Church could now be petitioned by a taxpayer to be sent to another church.

Also, establishment was not required by the second charter. Presumably, if the sentiment of the rulers and/or the citizens changed, the status of Congregationalism could change. Support for the Congregational Church, however, was broad and secure throughout the century, and as time passed the Mathers appeared to have been correct.[15] As the eighteenth century dawned the Congregationalists were once again confident that if they could keep the terms of the charter, the millennium was imminent.

The Enlightenment and the English Constitution

Despite the Mathers' protests to the contrary, the Charter of 1691 began a new era in Massachusetts politics, and this raises many questions. Why did this shift occur? Why was the clergy so easily persuaded or predisposed to accept it? One reason may be political fatigue. As we have seen, in the preceding decades ministers and magistrates were having increasing difficulty inculcating piety and virtue, and their desire to fully enforce the Puritan constitution may have been waning. More important, however, the winds of the Enlightenment were blowing new ideas to Massachusetts. Given their political problems, the ministers appeared to be open to an

14. Stout, *New England Soul,* 119.
15. Bonomi, *Under the Cope,* 93–121.

approach toward religion and politics inspired by the Enlightenment and the English Constitution.

On the face of it, it is remarkable that an intellectual movement so contradictory to Puritan thought would tempt the Congregationalists. As Carl Becker's summary of the essential articles of the Enlightenment indicates, the gap between the Puritans and the philosophes was great: Man is not natively depraved; the end of life is life itself; man, guided solely by the light of reason and experience, is capable of perfecting the good life on earth; and the first and essential condition of the good life on earth is the freeing of men's minds from the bonds of ignorance and superstition and their bodies from the arbitrary oppression of the constituted social authorities.[16]

The problem ministers faced lay in their deep commitment to the unity of reason and revelation.

> One of the most interesting features of the sermons before 1763, as well as afterwards, is the treatment of the law of nature. By this is meant the general principles of justice and equity under which men were conceived to have lived just before the founding of any society or civil state and which gave men therefore their so called "natural rights". This law had been planted by God deep in the hearts of men, "written as with a pen of iron and the point of a diamond", before the fuller revelation of the written law, and was still to be found there. There seems little evidence that the clergy, at least, thought of it as distinct from the law of God. Rather it gained greater force as a part of God's law. Thus in 1669 John Davenport in his Election Sermon said, "the Law of Nature is God's law." Again and again the clergy made this assertion and clearly regarded the laws of nature as sacredly and legally binding as any other part of the divine law. . . . John Barnard in his Massachusetts Election Sermon of 1734 phrased it somewhat differently but with equal assurance: "This Voice of Nature is the Voice of God."[17]

Their commitment to reason caused the Congregationalists little difficulty in the seventeenth century, since they had developed an elaborate synthesis between reason and revelation.[18] However, when the Enlightenment transformed the world of reason, the Congregationalists experienced difficulty. "Rationalist by training and temper, the ministers

16. Carl Becker, *The Heavenly City of the Eighteenth-Century Philosophers*, 102–3.
17. Alice M. Baldwin, *New England Clergy and the American Revolution*, 14–15.
18. Norman Fiering does a marvelous job of describing the Pre-Cartesian synthesis developed at Harvard and chronicling its demise in *Moral Philosophy at Seventeenth-Century Harvard: A Discipline in Transition.*

found it hard to argue against a secular doctrine which seemed to have preempted the field of reason. Often they attempted to meet the new philosophy on its 'own terms,' without realizing that he who defines the terms defines the debate."[19]

That the Enlightenment represented a challenge to Congregational-ist theology is not surprising. Believing wholeheartedly that "all truth is God's truth," and accepting the new arguments as reasonable, the ministers had no choice but to try and develop a new synthesis.

> The most pervasive intellectual change was the withdrawal of God from His place in the forefront of all thinking. God continued to exert a powerful influence but from a seemingly greater distance. New Englanders of the eighteenth century felt His hand less heavily and less constantly upon them than their fathers had done. They thought more about the way He shook the earth or moved the waters, and less about why He afflicted His chosen people by doing so. And as they became more interested in His handiwork than in His judgements they grew less concerned about their standing with Him. The seventeenth century, overwhelmed with a sense of human depravity, had worried about how to control the corrupt will. . . . The eighteenth century was ready, for certain limited purposes at least, to "waive the consideration of man's moral turpitude." In thinking about the state, there was less preoccupation with controlling the depravity of subjects and more with controlling that of the rulers; there was less thought of reducing the people's offensiveness to God, more of reducing the ruler's possible offensiveness to the people.[20]

Of all aspects of their worldview, the Congregationalists' political thought was particularly vulnerable to the Enlightenment, since, outside of Old Testament law, the Puritans did not believe that Scripture spoke directly about politics. They had always been open to extra-scriptural input in this area, so being open to the latest ideas about politics was not new. Clearly, the clergy as well as the citizens of Massachusetts had been considering the new thinking about politics during the last half of the seventeenth century; hence, when an opportunity came in the Glorious Revolution to reestablish the original charter, it was not for them a radical decision to refashion their political system in accordance with these new ideas.

Ironically, the worst fears of John Winthrop were realized. Rather than Massachusetts being the vehicle to transform Europe, Europe was

19. McWilliams, *The Idea,* 157.
20. Morgan, *Puritan Political Ideas,* xxxv.

changing Massachusetts. What is even more remarkable, seemingly no one noticed. As long as Congregationalists understood themselves to be committed to reason and revelation, and as long as they upheld the covenant, they perceived themselves to be in accord with their Puritan fathers. Reason indicated that European society, and especially English society, had a lot to offer, and they felt compelled to take advantage of what they could.

According to Harry Stout, the Enlightenment quickly manifested itself in the lives of Massachusetts Congregationalist ministers and citizens through the process of *anglicanization*. Through this process society began to embrace many of the manners, habits, tastes, and social ideas of the British aristocracy.

> The age of Cotton Mather, Urian Oakes, Jr., and Thomas Shepard III was also the age of Newton, Locke, Addison, and Tillotson. No well-read provincial could escape the excitement these luminaries were generating in science, literature, epistemology, and ethics; nor could they resist English influence in dress, speech, literary style, or architecture. For New England elites, England supplied standards of urbanity, sophistication, and broad-mindedness to be emulated for both intellectual and social reasons.[21]

Through anglicanization, Congregational ministers, along with the rest of the elite, came to view their relationship to England in very positive terms.

The process of anglicanization also extended to politics. The Congregationalists were particularly open to incorporating the political thinking and practices of Europe. "Anglicization operated as a political force reshaping institutions of law and government to conform to English practice."[22] Foremost within the political framework assimilated by the clergy was the English Constitution. Technically, the ministers embraced only the principles on which it was based, but in reality it became their political identity. As Alice Baldwin points out,

> to the New England ministers the government of Great Britain after 1688 and of their own colonies came nearest to their ideal of what government should be. . . . Under William III and the Georges the English government was, they thanked God, not arbitrary but legal, a mixed government in which the prerogatives of sovereign and people mutually supported each other, a government with the best constitution

21. Stout, *New England Soul*, 128.
22. Ibid., 127.

in the world, formed on common reason, common consent, and common good, by which the rights and liberties of the people were carefully guarded and the rulers were bound by the law.[23]

It is important to note that under the phrase *English Constitution* the ministers included almost every political idea important to them, whether it was actually a part of the English Constitution or not. Clinton Rossiter outlines the English Constitution as committed to liberty, classical virtue, natural law, English rights (Magna Charta), balanced government, habeas corpus, limited monarchy, annual Parliaments, free elections, liberty of the press, and the blessing of learned and upright judges.[24] The ministers' understanding of it contained all these ideas and more, including a well-developed understanding of religious and civil liberty, and an emphasis on the importance of virtuous magistrates and citizens.

One reason for this may be the influence of Whig constitutional theory on the thinking of the clergy. Several scholars have illustrated the connection between the ministers and the Whigs. As H. Trevor Colbourn points out, "the sources cited by the divines in their sermons often read like a directory of 'true Whig' historians. The classical authors—Tacitus, Sallust (both in the Thomas Gordon translation), Plutarch, and Caesar— were closely followed by Locke and Sidney, Coke and Sommers, Burnet and Rapin."[25] Consequently, it is not surprising that the ministers often confused the English Constitution with what they and the Whigs wanted it to mean. This will become more apparent in chapter 4 when we analyze the sermons published prior to the Stamp Act.

The ministers not only consulted classical texts, they also reinterpreted Scripture to cohere with these new ideas.

> In the thirty-year period of formal peace that followed the Treaty of Utrecht (1713–1745), third-generation ministers completed the cultural and intellectual transition to a new Anglo-American world that began with the new charter. This transition required a reinterpretation of New England's past that emphasized the founders' love of civil and religious liberty, and wrote off intolerance as an error common to all respectable seventeenth-century societies. As the eighteenth century

23. Baldwin, *New England Clergy*, 83.
24. Clinton Rossiter, *Seedtime of the Republic: The Origin of the American Tradition of Political Liberty*, 142–43.
25. H. Trevor Colbourn, *The Lamp of Experience: Whig History and the Intellectual Origins of the American Revolution*, 60.

wore on, however, it became more apparent that their own past was not the only past in need of revision. Because of the enduring hold of *Sola Scriptura* on New England's self-consciousness, anglicanization became as much an exegetical as an historical problem; one that involved rereading the Old Testament in light of current social and political realities. Just as ministers recalled aspects of their own past selectively to coincide with present circumstances and orthodoxies, so they now switched their emphasis in Old Testament preaching from Israel's "theocracy," where God intervened in the course of nature, to "Israel's Constitution" or to the civil laws and human instruments that God used to uphold his people without recourse to miraculous interventions.[26]

The degree to which the Congregationalists embraced English political thought can be seen in their preaching. John Wise incorporated it throughout his *Vindication of the Government of New England Churches*, in 1717:

> Wise considered man first in his natural state, enjoying the liberty which belonged to him, a liberty which made him subject to no other human being. In consequence, all men in this state were equal in authority and each had a right to judge for himself what was most conducive to his happiness and welfare. This liberty and equality of men, so Wise believed, could not be lessened until, in order to form a civil state, they gave up certain rights, at the same time preserving and cherishing as much as was consistent with the public good. The people were, therefore, the original of all power, but when they combined in society they delegated a part of their power and authority to others. . . . He concluded that a democracy was the type of government which the "light of nature" often directed men toward. "A democracy, This is a form of government, which the light of nature does highly value, and often directs to, as most agreeable to the just and natural prerogative of human beings."[27]

Jonathan Mayhew, considered one of the most influential Congregationalists of the eighteenth century and by some as a "father" of the American Revolution,[28] drew heavily on Whig thinking.

> From almost any perspective it is difficult to view the Lockean arguments of Mayhew's *Discourse on Unlimited Submission* as an early espousal of the ideology of the American Revolution. His assault on the notions

26. Stout, *New England Soul*, 166.
27. Baldwin, *New England Clergy*, 28–29.
28. See, for instance, John Wingate Thornton, ed., *The Pulpit of the American Revolution: or, the Political Sermons of the Period of 1776*.

of the divine right of kings and passive obedience was phrased as a defense of the prevailing British constitution—and, more specifically, of the Glorious Revolution. In fact, though Mayhew was clearly familiar with Locke, the bulk of his doctrines (and much of his language) was "borrowed" from the tracts of Benjamin Hoadley.[29]

It is important to note that although ministers embraced Whig thought, there was a considerable debate concerning its precise meaning. T. H. Breen characterizes the debate as taking place between "the Court" and "the Country." These were two political movements, each composed of members of the Congregational clergy, that surfaced almost immediately after the Glorious Revolution and existed in tension throughout most of the eighteenth century. Both movements embraced the principles of the English Constitution, but understood them in different ways. Members of the "Court" desired a more aristocratic political system. They believed in a hierarchical society in which citizens were deferential to rulers. They emphasized those aspects of the constitution that could be understood to encourage hierarchy, order, and tradition, and to discourage pure democracy, anarchy, and revolution.

The "Country" saw in the English Constitution support for a more liberal democratic society. Its adherents viewed government as a corrupting force and saw that the greatest virtue in society can be found in the people as a whole. They were not Levellers but believed in a greater degree of social equality, sovereignty of the people, and the active role of the people in government through frequent elections. They also wanted the franchise expanded to include more property owners and believed that citizens can be trusted with the right to revolution.[30]

The debate between these groups came to a head in 1705 when a ministers' convention proposed a modification of church government advocated by members of the "Court." They recommended that standing councils be put in place that would have authority over the churches in their areas. Like the Saybrook proposals that were eventually adopted in Connecticut, these recommendations would have moved Massachusetts Congregationalism in a decidedly Presbyterian direction. Led by John Wise, the Country party defeated these proposals, but the disagreement which the debate represented continued throughout the eighteenth century.[31]

29. Heimert, *Religion*, 254.
30. Breen, *The Character,* 203–69.
31. Walker, *A History,* 201–11.

The influence of English thought was significant and at odds with Puritan political theology. For example, Rossiter finds that the colonist who embraced the political theory of the English Constitution "was more than likely to subscribe to . . . the concept of man as an essentially good, sociable, educable creature; the historical or logical state of nature; the formation of society and government through an act of will, specifically through the technique of compact or contract; 'peace and Security,' 'the Publick Good,' 'the Happiness of the people,' and 'the preservation of the natural Rights of Mankind' as the chief ends of government."[32] Although common ground between the English and Puritan constitutions can be found, they are clearly distinct. The Puritan founders would never have accepted the enlightened view of human nature and politics implied in the English Constitution. Neither would they have accepted the expansion of citizenship beyond the visible saints or the emphasis on a classical or Aristotelian notion of virtue.[33]

Nevertheless, despite the changes found in the second charter, as the eighteenth century progressed the clergy became increasingly comfortable with it. The ministers remained the conscience of the colony. Through the jeremiads, the citizens were continually reminded that Massachusetts was still a "Citty upon a Hill," and its citizens could, through obedience and virtue, be used by God to complete the Reformation. In an interpretational shift reminiscent of twentieth-century United States Supreme Court jurisprudence, the Congregationalist clergy now emphasized the spirit of the Puritan founders, rather than their original intent. The divine history of New England was reconceived as a progressive unfolding of God's desire for New England and the world in accordance with the Enlightened notions of religious freedom and Protestant tolerance.

The Congregational clergy quickly came to understand that the second charter represented an improvement over the founders' vision and revised its historiography accordingly. "Henceforth, the founders would be officially remembered not for their intolerance (now an embarrassing episode of misguided zeal) but for their heroic defense of religious and civil liberty."[34] Nathan Hatch illustrates this well.

> In 1754 Mayhew articulated the form of the myth, which would become standard for the following generation. "Our ancestors," he

32. Rossiter, *Seedtime*, 142.
33. Fiering, *Moral Philosophy*, 10–62.
34. Stout, *New England Soul*, 119.

declared, "tho' not perfect and infallible in all respects, were a religious, brave and virtuous set of men, whose love of liberty, civil and religious, brought them from their native land, into the American deserts." By the end of the French and Indian War this grafting of Whig political values onto traditional conceptions of New England's collective identity was virtually complete. In his thanksgiving sermon for the victory at Quebec Samuel Cooper reflected on New England's history and surmised that his progenitors had transplanted themselves into the wilds of America because they were "smitten with a Love of Liberty, and possessed with an uncommon Reverence to the Dictates of Conscience."[35]

The justification for this shift was made on the grounds that God's continued blessing of New England signaled his pleasure with its new direction, as well as his intention that it continue. Nevertheless, the jeremiad still contained its biting warning and call to piety and virtue.

> While eighteenth century occasional rhetoric minimalized Israel's miracles and persecutions, it retained the familiar litany of Israel's sins and judgments, meant as a solemn warning and mirror of New England's own endangered status. Even in the excitement of centennial celebration, the people must not forget the sobering truth that they had "done worse and worse in every generation," and thus stood even closer to divine desertion. This . . . was in spite of the fact that the "faithful ministers" had not flagged in their proclamation of the will of God. The warning was harsh, but in a twist of logic perfected by his predecessors, Prince turned it into a ringing affirmation of New England's greatness. Despite fallings-away in the faith, there was a core of faithful ministers and pious church members who ensured the continuation of covenant protections.[36]

If this core would but continue and grow, the reward would be not only the completion of the Reformation, but also the inauguration of the long-awaited millennium promised in the Bible.[37]

Although the anglicanization of the Congregationalist clergy was extensive, its importance must not be exaggerated. England and its political ideas mattered to the clergy, but the clergy did not become mere mirrors of English or Whig thought. Jack P. Greene advises that when examining the European contribution to colonial thought, we should not overlook the unique attributes of colonial thought.[38] Greene's advice applies to

35. Hatch, *Sacred*, 46.
36. Stout, *New England Soul*, 174.
37. Hatch, *Sacred*, 21–54.
38. Jack P. Greene, *The Intellectual Construction of America: Exceptionalism and Identity from 1492 to 1800.*

these ministers. The Massachusetts Congregationalists were influenced by England but developed a political thought with exceptional characteristics. They altered, modified, and recast Puritan thinking, but they did not divorce themselves from it.

One of the biggest differences between Congregationalist and Whig thought had to do with the clergy's insistence on the importance of religion for politics. While the clergy adopted ideas that appeared to minimize the role of religion in government, its members *never* regarded themselves to be involved in secularization. They still held that religion was the foundation of life and politics. They had merely adopted a new approach toward government. Under it they believed Christianity would flourish, thus producing the pious and virtuous citizens needed to keep the covenant. Although spirituality was less important to government in the new regime, and though the Congregationalists were more optimistic about the power of reason to promote virtuous behavior than the Puritans, religion was still regarded as important to politics because of the essential role it played in fostering virtue.

What kept Congregationalist political identity unique was the covenant. It provided an identity and purpose separate from England and its constitution. Although the ministers respected both, they were capable of being critical of both when necessary. Moreover, when relations with England deteriorated in the founding era, the ministers could cast aside their attachment to the English Constitution, because their political theory, though influenced by the Whigs, was their own. As Harry Stout points out, "England's constitution was illustrative, not determinative, of political thought in the New England pulpit. Its provisions duplicated and clarified truths already established in ancient Israel and practiced in seventeenth-century New England."[39]

The Great Awakening and the War with France

Massachusetts Congregationalist political thought from the enactment of the second charter to 1760 can be understood on the whole as the gradual and progressive development of a unique synthesis of Enlightenment thinking with Puritan theology and history. Although understanding this is essential for understanding Congregationalist political thought of the founding era, it is also important to be aware of two eighteenth-century historical events: the Great Awakening and the French and Indian War.

39. Stout, *New England Soul*, 171.

The Great Awakening was a colony-wide spiritual revival. It emerged ostensibly through the preaching of revivalist and evangelical ministers such as George Whitefield.[40] In Massachusetts it first surfaced in Northhampton at Jonathan Edwards's church, and during the next decade, the Awakening brought out theological divisions that had been latent among Massachusetts Congregationalists for some time.

The Awakening divided Massachusetts Congregationalists into two primary camps: the Old Lights who opposed the doctrine and method of the Awakening, and the New Lights who were supporters. The dispute centered primarily over the relationship between reason and will. The Old Lights were uncomfortable with a movement they perceived as being rooted in enthusiasm and emotion but not reason. They were sympathetic to the Enlightenment, and "their most distinguishing intellectual mark was the notion that man is—or should be—a rational being, one who derives his standards of virtuous behavior from an observation of the external world."[41] They called themselves "liberals" and believed that faith was bred best in an environment of reason rather than emotion.

In contrast, the New Lights were uncomfortable with the rationalist direction of the Enlightenment. They were not anti-intellectual but downplayed the priority of reason by giving the affections a more crucial role in their epistemology. The New Lights asserted that regeneration was not merely an intellectual event but also an affair of the heart and required the "inward operation of the Holy Spirit." In addition, they argued that "virtue [was] dependent on the reception of a 'vital indwelling principle from the Holy Spirit.' "[42] Both sides argued for the importance of virtue but were separated in their understanding of the role and importance of reason.

The Great Awakening and the intellectual debate surrounding it clearly influenced Massachusetts Congregationalism during the founding era, though there is some debate about its importance for politics. Alan Heimert argues that the Great Awakening created a division that continued to exist among the Congregational clergy throughout the founding. He sees that Congregationalism remained divided into two camps that embraced different political agendas. The Old Lights had a more conservative, pro-British perspective; the New Lights had a more democratic, liberal perspective.

40. Winthrop S. Hudson, *American Protestantism*, 31.
41. Heimert, *Religion*, 5.
42. Ibid., 6.

Until and unless Liberals were confronted by imperial issues, their interpretations of the social contract, particularly as they applied to the internal affairs of the provinces, were careful and methodical arguments for the holding in check a populace that was by no means conceived to be a community of natural equals. . . . They preached Locke almost as a justification of the status quo, and even more importantly they did so by way of deploring and seeking to subdue the revolutionary enthusiasm that was, despite their hopes and efforts, arising in the American populace.

It was the more orthodox clergymen of America who infused the Lockean vocabulary with a moral significance, a severity and an urgency, and thereby translated the ideas of social contract and natural law into a spur to popular activity.[43]

William G. McLoughlin sees the Awakening impacting the founding by creating in the New Lights and their followers an egalitarian theology and a habit of ecclesiastical self-government that prepared people for self-government. It also created a psychology that permitted revolution. McLoughlin, as well as Heimert, finds that the Old Lights were too committed to the English government and too fearful of democracy to have adequately supported the Revolution.[44]

Although there were many differences between Old and New Lights, there is virtually no difference in the political sermons of the two groups. As Heimert points out, "if the discourses of the ministry were assessed only in terms of the extent to which each at some point repeated the postulates of John Locke, Liberals and Calvinists—with several signal exceptions— would appear nearly indistinguishable."[45]

Indeed, Steven Weber, in his study of eighteenth-century sermons, discovered that rural New Light political preaching was infused with the same Whig ideology used in the Old Light pulpits of Boston.[46] Such evidence has led Nathan Hatch to comment,

Historians of religion in eighteenth-century New England unfortunately . . . have missed the most towering feature before them, the overwhelming political unity of the Congregational clergy. Despite ongoing doctrinal debate, clergymen across the entire theological spectrum followed a singular path of political logic in espousing the cause of

43. Ibid., 16–17.
44. McLoughlin, "Enthusiasm for Liberty."
45. Heimert, *Religion,* 16–17
46. Weber, *Rhetoric and History,* 91–112.

Britain against France, America against Britain, and Federalism against the Democratic Republicans.[47]

Despite their theological differences, Massachusetts Congregationalist ministers spoke with remarkable harmony in the area of politics. While the categories of rural/urban, Old Light/New Light, trinitarian/unitarian may be useful for isolating various areas of difference among clergy members on a number of issues, they do not apply to their political thought. The ministers present a political vision of remarkable consistency and coherence, and, on those occasions where exceptions exist, the differences cannot adequately be explained by these or other categories.

An event that had far more political significance for this era was the French and Indian War. New Englanders believed that if France gained control of New England, their divine experiment would be over. France would take away their religious and civil liberties and impose a papal and monarchical tyranny.

> The ministers' rhetoric associated France inseparably with "the merciless Rage of *Popish* power" and evoked images of the inquisition, the fury of Queen Mary, the schemes of the Stuarts, and the more recent suppression of Protestants in France. Roman Catholicism represented for New Englanders not only their ancestors' most hated foe but also an immediate conspiracy against the liberties of all mankind. Typical of this mood was the fear expressed . . . that "our inveterate and *popish* Enemies both without and within the Kingdom, are restless to enslave and ruin us." If France won the struggle, "Cruel *Papists* would quickly fill the *British Colonies,* seize our Estates, abuse our Wives and Daughters, and barbarously murder us; as they have done the like in *France* and *Ireland.*"[48]

Consequently, the war took on an Armageddon level of importance for the clergy:

> In this war, as others, they encouraged armed conflict for nationalistic and prophetic reasons. . . . [T]hey had to establish the justness and necessity of war with France in terms drawn both from secular writings on civil liberties and property rights, and from Scripture prophesies foretelling terrible wars between God's new Israel and the forces of the Antichrist.[49]

47. Hatch, *Sacred,* 6–7.
48. Ibid., 38.
49. Stout, *New England Soul,* 244.

Probably at no other time was it more important to be identified with England. "In sermon after sermon they lifted up the standard of British liberty against the aggressive tyranny of Roman Catholicism."[50]

When it became apparent in 1759 that the war was won, English patriotism was fervent. The euphoria of victory is reflected in the sermons that appear at the beginning of Part II. The celebration, however, was short-lived. England's substantial war debt brought legislation that provoked a profound political confrontation with the colonies. In the matter of a decade the clergy would be required to rework a political theory they had spent the century refining. However, before the role of the ministers in the revolutionary era can be fully understood, their education and place in parish and colony life must be examined.

50. Hatch, *Sacred,* 49.

3

A COVENANT FOR LIFE
THE MINISTERS, THEIR
EDUCATION, AND THEIR PARISH

The ministerial office in eighteenth-century New England, then, was inseparable from the fabric of the New England towns that contained it. But what gave this ministerial presence and office such importance—what, in short, lay behind the ideal and practice of permanence—was the minister's role as the mainstay of communal order. There was, in fact, little in congregationalist ecclesiastical theory that demanded lifetime pastorates: permanence, rather, was a requirement of the social order of the New England town. The most distinctive feature of eighteenth-century New England society and culture was communalism, a social structure and ideology in which order, harmony, and obedience to all authority were the highest public and social values.

Donald M. Scott

The political thought of the Massachusetts Congregationalist clergy during the founding era is important because the minister was an individual of extraordinary power and influence. The Congregationalist clergy was the single most influential group in the colony, and the minister was usually the most educated and respected member of the parish.[1] The ministry often attracted the best and brightest candidates. The Puritans were committed to an educated and learned ministry and founded Harvard College as a seminary shortly after they arrived. Although the eighteenth-century Congregationalist Church did not have the monopoly on quality individuals that it had in the seventeenth century, now having to share Harvard graduates with other occupations, "the ministry still continued to attract a solid proportion of the very best college graduates from the

---

1. Baldwin, *New England Clergy,* 3–12.

same middle and upper class families that had always supplied sons to the church."[2]

While the power and prestige associated with the office of minister certainly had secular appeal, the decision to enter the ministry entailed more than personal preference. For the most part, occupational choices were not the personal decision of the students. As Donald M. Scott states:

> Essentially, a young man was selected out for the ministry, and here the passive voice is used deliberately. Young men of the eighteenth century generally did not play a very active role in determining their adult occupations and stations. The basic decision lay with parents and elders, who tried to equip their sons for a position commensurate with family tradition, and standing, resources, and, to an extent, the son's particular traits and talents. But the young man going into the ministry had a particularly acute sense that divine agency was at work placing him in the sacred office.[3]

Neither were educational choices left to the candidate. A college education was required. Virtually all Massachusetts Congregationalist ministers from the founding era were college graduates, with a huge majority having been educated at Harvard.[4] A few from the western region of the colony were Yale graduates, but Harvard was clearly the dominant intellectual influence for ministers and the colony.

Reflecting Puritan pedagogy, a Harvard education was classically oriented. This is apparent in the entrance requirements, which in 1734 included the ability "ex tempore to read, construe and parse Tully, Virgil, or Such like common classical Latin Authors; and to write true Latin in Prose, and to be Skill'd in making Latin verse, or at Least in the rules of Prosodia; and to read, construe and parse ordinary Greek, as in the New Testament, Isocrates, or such like, and decline the Paradigms of Greek Nouns and Verbs."[5]

Depending on their economic status, prospective students received this training in one of two ways. The wealthier students, such as Samuel Cooper, attended a preparatory school, whereas poorer students, such as John Cleaveland, received tutoring from their college-educated parish

2. Bonomi, *Under the Cope*, 71.

3. Donald M. Scott, *From Office to Profession: The New England Ministry, 1750–1850*, 7–8.

4. Harry Price Kerr, "The Character of Political Sermons Preached at the Time of the American Revolution," 11.

5. Samuel Eliot Morison, *Three Centuries of Harvard, 1636–1936*, 103.

minister.[6] Age, however, was not an obstacle. Many students entered Harvard in their early teens. Jonathan Mayhew entered at nineteen, an advanced age for new students. Of the class admitted in 1740, for instance, "the average age . . . was about sixteen."[7]

Because the undergraduate curriculum was the same for every student, some, such as Jonathan Mayhew, did not make career choices until the conclusion of their senior year, after which they returned for more education. Almost all ministry prospects returned to Harvard to pursue a master's degree in divinity.

Harvard's express purpose was to train students to lead "Sober, righteous, & godly Lives." Nevertheless, the behavior of the students was not unlike that of teenagers of any era. As Charles Akers recounts, "they shot firecrackers in the yard at night, made 'indecent Noises' at all times, stole chickens from neighboring farmers, and sometimes took part in what was described in the Faculty Records as an 'Extravagent drinking Frolick.' " Moreover, the behavior of those students training for the ministry was virtually indistinguishable from others'. The biographical sketches of all Harvard students until 1771 written by J. L. Sibley and Clifford Shipton are filled with stories of future clergymen misbehaving as frequently as the future members of America's intellectual, political, and economic elite.[8]

A full understanding of the intellectual roots of Congregationalist political thought would require a comprehensive knowledge of the clergy's Harvard education. Unfortunately, little research has been done into intellectual life at eighteenth-century Harvard. The research of Perry Miller and Norman Fiering focuses on the seventeenth century. Daniel Walker Howe's work on moral philosophy at Harvard begins in the nineteenth century. Samuel Eliot Morison, the historian of Harvard, has written extensively on seventeenth-century Harvard and to some degree on nineteenth- and twentieth-century Harvard but only briefly touched on the eighteenth century.[9] According to Harvard historian George

6. Akers, *Divine Politician*, 7; Christopher M. Jedrey, *The World of John Cleaveland: Family and Community in Eighteenth-Century New England*, 19.

7. Charles W. Akers, *Called unto Liberty: A Life of Jonathan Mayhew, 1720–1766*, 22.

8. Ibid., 24; see also Clifford K. Shipton, *Sibley's Harvard Graduates: Biographical Sketches of Those Who Attended Harvard College*, vols. 4–16; and J. L. Sibley, *Biographical Sketches of Graduates of Harvard University*, vols. 1–4.

9. Fiering, *Moral Philosophy;* Norman Fiering, *Jonathan Edwards's Moral Thought and Its British Context;* Miller, *Errand*, 9; Miller, *New England Mind: Seventeenth Century;* Perry Miller, *The New England Mind: From Colony to Province;* Daniel Walker

Hunston Williams, Morison intended to do a work on the eighteenth century but never completed the project.

Thomas Jay Siegel has done the best research in this area. Unfortunately, due to a lack of source material, Siegel cannot answer some questions about the ministers' education. Lecture notes were not published, and relatively few notes are found in student diaries. Some reading lists are available, but no records exist of what the students actually read or, more important, their reactions. Much of the problem stems from the Harvard library fire in 1764 that destroyed countless valuable records.

Siegel has, however, uncovered the general outline of undergraduate education at that time. "A freshman class was turned over to a tutor, who for four years guided the young scholars progressively through the classics, rhetoric, logic, natural philosophy, geography, ethics, divinity, metaphysics, mathematics, and astronomy. The tutor assigned readings and disputations, and sometimes encouraged his students to read independently in the library."[10]

It is important to note that divinity was a major part of every student's education. Their education "included the careful study and analysis of the Bible in the original tongues, a short handbook of Protestant divinity (Ames's *Medulla* or Wolleb's *Abridgement of Christian Divinity*), taking notes on two sermons every Lord's Day, and being quizzed on them subsequently."[11] For instance, John Winthrop, the future Hollis Professor of Mathematics, kept a diary of notes of every Lord's Day sermon he heard while a student because he would be expected to be able to reproduce them for his tutor.

Tutors were assisted by the college president, who was active in teaching, particularly in the area of divinity. The students' education was augmented in 1721 by the appointment of Edward Wigglesworth as the Hollis Professor of Divinity and in 1728 by the appointment of Isaac Greenwood as the Hollis Professor of Mathematics and Natural Philosophy. With these appointments, the tutor remained the coordinator and primary educator, deferring to these gentlemen in their areas of expertise.

Howe, *The Unitarian Conscience: Harvard Moral Philosophy, 1805–1861;* Samuel Eliot Morison, *The Founding of Harvard College.*

10. Thomas Jay Siegel, "Governance and Curriculum at Harvard College in the 18th Century," 26–27.

11. Edward G. Griffin, *Old Brick: Charles Chauncy of Boston, 1705–1787,* 20; see also Siegel, "Governance," 227.

In 1767, however, the tutorial system was revised. At this point the four tutors were reassigned to their own areas of expertise.

> To one was assigned all instruction in Latin; to another, Greek; to a third, Logic, Metaphysics, and Ethics; to a fourth, Natural Philosophy, Mathematics, Geography, and Astronomy; and all four taught Rhetoric, Elocution, and English composition. . . . The Hollis Professor of Divinity took charge of religious instruction, and [the Professor of Mathematics and Natural Philosophy] continued to deliver his lectures . . . in Natural Science.[12]

At no point in the eighteenth century was politics a part of the curriculum; nevertheless it was taught in several ways. First, political knowledge was a curricular by-product.

> The political knowledge that most students gained from their courses did not, then, come directly. Rather it appeared as a by-product of the student's constant immersions in the Greek and Roman classics and relatively brief exposure to ethics as a subdivision of moral philosophy. . . .
> The consequence was that many students read extensively in the Greek and Roman authors. Principal among them were Aristotle, Catullus, Cicero, Florus, Hesiod, Homer, Horace, Isocrates, Livy, Sallust, Sophocles, Virgil, and Xenophon. What is striking about this group of authors is that . . . many of them included political commentary in their writings.[13]

Second, and more significant, the students learned politics at Harvard through extracurricular means. Siegel discovered that students were exposed to political ideas of a more modern nature through the "informal curriculum," beginning in the 1720s.[14] The informal curriculum, as described in student diaries, comprised those books students read either on their own on the "unofficial" advice of a tutor or as a member of a secret society. Siegel found the formal curriculum was somewhat politicized. Harvard was under close scrutiny from the community, and, due to the conservative nature of Massachusetts, there was often a lag time between library acquisition of a book and its inclusion in the curriculum.

> Despite the increasing intellectual openness of New England society and innovations in the College's formal instruction, Harvard's curriculum always lagged behind the developments in the transformation of

12. Morison, *Three Centuries,* 90.
13. David W. Robson, *Educating Republicans: The College in the Era of the Revolution, 1750–1800,* 15–16.
14. Siegel, "Governance," chap. 6.

> knowledge that were occurring in England and Europe during the
> late seventeenth and early eighteenth centuries. As a consequence new
> books and ideas came to New England and the College faster than the
> College officials could screen them and select the best ones to adopt,
> or assimilate, into the assigned readings.[15]

The faculty and students were aware of these books and new ideas and
were eager to study them.

The few existing Harvard library catalog records, student diary entries,
and bookseller records indicate that the political works of Locke, Sidney,
Pufendorf, Grotius, Milton, and Montesquieu were available to students,
some at least as early as 1726.[16] Moreover, Siegel finds that Harvard students formed secret societies throughout the eighteenth century, many of
which had an academic nature and were likely a source of political ideas
and discussions. One example is the debating club known as the Society
in Harvard College, organized by future minister Charles Chauncy in the
early 1720s. Another is the Speaking Club of 1770. If the latter group is any
measure, significant extracurricular reading and discussion of political
ideas occurred in these societies.[17]

Further evidence of the extent and political nature of the informal curriculum has been provided by Minor Myers Jr.'s research into eighteenth-
century Harvard master's questions.

> Presentation of a "quaestio" at commencement three years after taking
> the A.B. was the only academic exercise required for the degree of
> Master of Arts. . . . The process by which the questions were chosen
> remains largely unknown. Clearly, students had a hand in selecting
> them, but it fell to the president to approve both the questions and the
> positions to be argued. . . . Topics were usually tied to a candidate's
> chosen profession, especially if he intended to be a physician, minister,
> or lawyer.[18]

Myers found that one of the key sources these students used for choosing and preparing questions pertaining to politics was *Quaestiones Philo-
sophicae* by Thomas Johnson. Among the sources that Johnson instructed

    15. Ibid., 274.
    16. Elizabeth Carroll Reilly, "The Wages of Piety: The Boston Book Trade of
Jeremy Condy," 83–131.
    17. Albert Goodhue Jr., "The Reading of Harvard Students, 1770–1781, as
Shown by the Records of the Speaking Club"; and Griffin, *Old Brick*, 21–22.
    18. Minor Myers Jr., "A Source for Eighteenth-Century Harvard Master's
Questions"; see also Mary Latimer Gambrell, *Ministerial Training in Eighteenth-
Century New England.*

to be used in preparing questions are: Hugo Grotius, *De Jure Belli ac Pacis;* Samuel Pufendorf, *De Jure Naturae et Gentium;* Algernon Sidney, *Discourses Concerning Government;* John Locke, *Two Treatises of Government;* John Milton, *Pro Populo Anglicano Defensio;* Benjamin Hoadley, *The Origin and Institution of Civil Government;* Thomas Hobbes, *Leviathan;* Sir Robert Filmer, *Patriarcha;* and the *Freeholder's Grand Inquest.* Although we do not know which sources, if any, students actually consulted in preparing their questions, Myers argues that students, including those studying for the ministry, had access to these sources and utilized them.[19]

Given the insights offered by Siegel's research into the informal curriculum, and given the fact that virtually all ministers were master's-prepared, it is almost certain that many of them had extended exposure to the most current political thought of the eighteenth century.

Life in the Parish

Following graduation, ministerial candidates were eligible to receive a call to a parish. The Cambridge Platform established that the responsibility for calling, ordaining, and settling a minister lay entirely with the local congregation. While various ministerial associations were formed to examine candidates and "advise" parishes, the final decision was made by each congregation. Because ministers routinely spent their entire lifetimes in one parish, the minister and parish took considerable care in making a decision, as the call could not be broken by either party without mutual consent or just cause.

> Churches almost never called a man without a period of probationary preaching that usually lasted a minimum of three months, and often demanded a second or third stint before finally offering the candidate a "call." It was not at all uncommon for churches to try out a succession of candidates before agreeing on the one they wanted to "settle." . . .
>
> The candidates themselves were no less scrupulous, knowing full well that if they accepted a call, they were likely to be stuck with the situation the rest of their lives. They were equally aware of the capacities of contentious parishioners and faction-ridden communities to inflict misery on their pastors by sabotaging the support of the community and withdrawing various supplemental forms of salary support. Thus, it was not uncommon for a young preacher to reject a number of calls before finally settling.[20]

19. Myers, "A Source," 261–64.
20. Scott, *From Office,* 4.

Despite extensive training, the ministers were not, on the whole, well compensated for their work.

> Sometimes they were given land, money, or some other special induce-
> ment to settle and were usually promised a salary which, when paid
> regularly and in specie, meant comfort at least. But frequently the salary
> was in arrears or paid in depreciated currency and at best was none too
> large to meet the demands of such a position. For the most part the
> ministers lived in small towns or smaller villages and stretched their
> salaries to the family needs by farming or by taking into their homes a
> few boys whom they fitted for college or trained for the ministry.[21]

Once settled, the minister assumed an office of power and respect.
The clergy's power was virtually unrivaled in seventeenth-century society,
and although ministers shared respect with other professionals during
the eighteenth century, they gained even more power from the second
charter than they had from the first. The second charter limited the
involvement of government in ecclesiastical affairs. Consequently, provided he had the respect of his parishioners, the minister held virtually
unrivaled power.[22]

Even though a Congregational minister could not be directly involved
in politics, his influence was significant. "The clergyman was both the
keeper and purveyor of the public culture, the body of fundamental
precepts and values that defined the social community, and an enforcer
of the personal values and decorum that sustained it."[23]

In no area did the minister have greater influence than in the Sunday
worship services, which were the primary vehicle of public communication throughout New England at this time. Though newspapers and
publishing were growing, access to the press was limited, particularly in
rural areas. Hence, the worship services held a central place in the social-
ization and education of the citizens of Massachusetts.[24] For instance, one

> Maine villager recalled that his minister's "long prayer was always inter-
> esting. For in it he told the congregation, through his address to the
> Almighty, the village news with great particularity. That prayer served
> all the purposes of a local newspaper. From it we learned of those who
> during the preceding week had been married, who were sick, who had

21. Baldwin, *New England Clergy*, 3.
22. Walker, *A History*, 249–50.
23. Scott, *From Office*, 12.
24. Richard D. Brown "Spreading the Word: Rural Clergymen and the Communication Network of 18th-Century New England," 2–4; Baldwin, *New England
Clergy*, 4.

died, who had gone on a journey, who had gone to college or come back from college."[25]

As a rule two worship services of considerable length were held each Sunday. The first began at nine in the morning and started with

> a prayer of "about a quarter of an houre" by the pastor. . . . Following the petition, the teacher read a passage of the Bible, expounding it section by section. . . . Next in order . . . came a psalm, lined off by the ruling elder, or where such an officer was lacking, by a brother . . . that the congregation might sing. . . . The psalm was always followed by the sermon, always esteemed the central element in the Congregational service. . . . After the sermon the teacher, when there was such an officer, or if there was not, then the pastor, made "a shorter Prayer," asking the divine blessing on the sermon; and the congregation was dismissed with the benediction.[26]

After an intermission of several hours during which the parishoners informally fellowshipped with one another, they would gather for a second service. Everyone was expected to attend both services; the second service was different in content, but employed the same basic format as the first.

The Sermon

Of all the political writing of the founding era, sermons provide us with a rare glimpse of both what the clergy thought and what a large majority of the citizens heard. No other surviving medium can so successfully provide this insight. Moreover, since virtually all of the extant political writing of the clergy consists of sermons, and as these are the primary focus of this study, this genre will be examined in some detail.

In keeping with Reformed tradition, the sermon was the central feature of the worship service and a minister's single most influential activity.[27]

> The average weekly churchgoer in New England (and there were far more churchgoers than church members) listened to something like seven thousand sermons in a lifetime, totaling somewhere around fifteen thousand hours of concentrated listening. These striking statistics become even more significant when it is recalled that until the last decade of the colonial era there were at the local level few, if any,

25. Brown, "Spreading the Word," 8. It should be noted that Maine was a part of Massachusetts until 1820.
26. Walker, *A History*, 238–41.
27. Bonomi, *Under the Cope*, 68.

competing public speakers offering alternative messages. For all intents
and purposes, the sermon was the only regular voice of authority.[28]

Despite having many opportunities to address political issues, the
ministers mostly refrained from doing so. They followed a very strict
tradition of addressing only spiritual issues on Sundays. Harry Price
Kerr found that "not only political matters were barred from religious
preaching. So also was explicit reference to any person, place, or event
which was part of the contemporary scene." Although we do know that
some ministers, such as Peter Whitney, violated this unwritten code, the
extent to which it was followed even through the turbulent times of the
Revolution is remarkable.[29]

The ministers refrained from addressing political issues on Sunday,
but they were able to address politics on other occasions. In keeping with
the Calvinist belief that all human activity falls under the jurisdiction of
God's Word, provision was made for the Word to be preached at every
significant event in the life of the community.[30] These occasions included
provincial or colonial election days, fast and thanksgiving days, artillery
elections, and anniversaries. It was in "occasional" sermons that political
issues and ideas were addressed, and ministers took full advantage of the
opportunity.

Although relatively few Congregationalist ministers had the opportunity to give election sermons, virtually all gave other forms of occasional
sermons. Between 1760 and 1790, Massachusetts Congregationalist ministers published over 130 election and occasional sermons pertaining to
politics, and more than 40 percent of Massachusetts and Connecticut
ministers between 1740 and 1800 published at least one.[31] It is through
these sermons that we can best glean the political thinking of Massachusetts Congregational ministers and ascertain the political ideas that
most Massachusetts citizens heard during the founding.

The Puritans not only had a strict code of what subject matter was
appropriate to a specific sermon, they also used the same general outline
for every sermon, regardless of the occasion. The sermon began with a
literal summary of the chosen text, followed by an explanation of the
lessons that could be drawn directly from it. The sermon concluded

28. Stout, *New England Soul,* 4.
29. Kerr, "The Character," 168, 26–28.
30. Stout, *New England Soul,* 27.
31. Hatch, *Sacred,* 177.

with an application of the text tailored to the present circumstances of society and the audience.[32] They so rigorously followed this form because, contrary to the theory of sermons espoused by the Church of England, which held that the purpose of the sermon was to "please and inspire," the Puritans, inheritors of a rational tradition, argued that a sermon was to "inform and convince." They "held that men must be encouraged to test the validity of a creed with their intellects. Only after conviction had been achieved in this manner could ministers safely inflame the passions as a spur to the will."[33] This form, scrupulously followed in virtually all sermons, had been deemed most effective for allowing a listener to judge the validity of a doctrine.

These occasions—election day, fast and thanksgiving days, artillery elections, and anniversaries—provided abundant opportunities for ministers to address a variety of political and social issues. Clearly, the most important source of political thinking was the election sermon. Beginning in 1634 on the first annual election day, when John Cotton tried to persuade the electors to reelect John Winthrop as Governor, one minister was selected annually to preach a sermon to the most politically and socially important members of the colony before the general court's yearly election of magistrates.[34]

Election day was a colony-wide holiday and attracted the colony's elite to Boston on the last Wednesday in May. "Election day began with cannon firing, military exercises, organization of the General Court, and a procession from the seat of government to a nearby church."[35] During the eighteenth century the size of the audience that would gather at the church to hear the sermon is estimated to have been between 175 and 750 people. At the very least, those in attendance usually included the 110 to 120 representatives of the towns, the outgoing General Council of 28 members, the governor and his staff, as well as many of Massachusetts's Congregational ministers whose annual convention always took place the following day in Boston.[36]

Just as every Congregationalist sermon followed a similar form, so almost every election sermon in the Revolutionary era had similar content.

32. Plumstead, *The Wall*, 31–34.
33. Kerr, "The Character," 132–34.
34. Lindsay Swift, "The Massachusetts Election Sermons," 389–90.
35. Kerr, "The Character," 38–39.
36. Plumstead, *The Wall*, 11; Kerr, "The Character," 39–43. Plumstead estimates 150–75 individuals attended the election sermon, while Kerr estimates 500–750.

Phraseology differed from one minister to another, of course, but the same ideas were set forth so consistently that they can be summarized quite briefly: Civil government originates in an agreement between men to establish a system which will promote the common good. Holy Scripture sets forth the best general maxims of government. From scripture we can see that government is necessary, but that God has not designated any particular form superior to others. Hence men may choose whichever form seems best suited to their peculiar circumstances. By the terms of their agreement the people pledge obedience to one or more rulers and the rulers promise in return to act for the good of all. The people are competent to judge the propriety of the actions of their rulers. So long as rulers act in their proper character, subjects must obey and cooperate with them, but if rulers act contrary to the terms of the agreement, the people not only may, but are in duty bound to resist. . . .

Advice addressed to groups in the audience was no less consistent from year to year than the main ideas. If the proper function of legislators was to act for the common good, nothing could better secure this goal than to promote virtue, suppress vice, and provide adequate financial support for ministers. Legislators should, moreover, choose councilors of proven wisdom, integrity, justice, and holiness, seek to redress the grievances of their constituents, and support the educational institutions of the colony.[37]

Even though the annual election sermon was heard by relatively few people, Martha Louise Counts is certainly correct to argue that it was the single most important form of political discourse in which Congregational ministers engaged.[38] Those selected to preach were Massachusetts's most respected clergy. In addition, the sermon was routinely printed by request under the direction of the government and circulated to, among others, all ministers in the colony. Not surprisingly, the ideas contained in an election sermon found their way during the coming years into other occasional sermons preached by ministers throughout Massachusetts.

The most common occasional sermons and the type heard by most Massachusetts parishioners were the fast and thanksgiving sermons. Unlike election sermons, these sermons were preached in every parish church throughout the state, usually several times a year, to a large audience. On fast days, citizens were mandated by law to congregate and hear about political and social issues and to seek God's favor. Although not every fast or thanksgiving day lent itself to political discourse, many did,

37. Kerr, "The Character," 50–52.
38. Counts, "Political Views," 3–4.

especially between 1763 and 1789. Moreover, the potential these sermons held for influencing the colony's citizens was not lost on politicians. They called for frequent days of fasting during the Revolution, with carefully worded proclamations they hoped would promote their cause.

> This was frequently the case during the revolution when "men like Jefferson, Hancock, and Sam Adams thus helped to make fasts and thanksgivings occasions on which their friends could preach 'sedition' and on which their enemies found it awkward to register effective opposition."[39]

Fast and thanksgiving days were the Puritan answer to the holy days of the Anglican Church. The Puritans took exception to the Catholic calendar; they believed it relegated the Sabbath to a day of secondary importance and frequently commemorated the wrong things. Nevertheless, they recognized that events sometimes warranted setting aside a day for prayer, fasting, and/or celebration.

> The most important—and ubiquitous—public ritual, however, was the fast, for it, more than any other ceremony, expressed the particular public consciousness of New England. Eighteenth-century New England possessed a remarkably coherent and self-conscious public culture that centered on the myth of its special providential founding and upon a deep sense of the exceptional character of its institutions and heritage. . . . God had called the Puritans to the wilderness to set up a model Christian commonwealth, and so long as New Englanders remained faithful to this charge, God would sustain and prosper them with special providential oversight. But if New England betrayed its charge, if its people fell into unruliness and its communities into disorder and conflict, and if its churches lost faith, a wrathful God would cast New England aside and punish it for its iniquity.[40]

Consequently, if public officials were persuaded that events indicated God's displeasure with Massachusetts, a day of fasting was called, during which the entire community was asked to consider their sin, pray for forgiveness, and to repent. A central part of the day would be a worship service in the parish church, during which the minister would preach a sermon related to the concerns expressed in the public proclamation. Frequently these sermons addressed political issues. Conversely, when events indicated that God had responded favorably, a day of thanksgiving was called and the same routine followed.

39. Kerr, "The Character," 86.
40. Scott, *From Office*, 13.

Another occasion on which political sermons were preached was the annual election of the Ancient and Honorable Artillery Company of Massachusetts. Established by John Winthrop in 1638, the company met once a year, and among pageantry, banquets, and military demonstrations, an election sermon was delivered prior to the election of officers. While only a few were published during the founding era, these sermons provide the best available statement on the ministers' reflections on war.

Political sermons were also preached at commemorative celebrations. On the whole these were not widespread in Massachusetts, and only twenty political sermons of this type were published between 1763 and 1783.[41] Nevertheless, some of the political events commemorated were the Landing at Plymouth, the Boston Massacre, the Battle of Lexington, and the Declaration of Independence.

As stated in the introduction, virtually all of the political writing done by the clergy consisted of sermons. Hence, for the most part, this is a study of published sermons. Stout and Hatch agree that for purposes of understanding political thought, going beyond published sermons to manuscript sermons is unnecessary. Published sermons represent the best available expression of Congregationalist political thinking. The publishing of sermons entailed significant expense, and hence they were carefully selected and prepared. Hatch actually argues for the priority of printed sermons:

> The great volume of sermons printed in Revolutionary America reflects anything but the arcane speculations of an isolated religious elite. The most likely sermons of all to be placed before the public were the very ones that received the heartiest "amen" among influential laymen. In other words, the printed sermons of Revolutionary New England are probably more representative of what was understood and believed in the pew than sermons that failed to arouse anyone's interest and thus were buried quietly in a minister's dusty file of manuscripts.[42]

The founding era "aroused the interests" of the colony in political thought, and the ministers responded with an outpouring of political sermons. In Part II we will examine how the clergy undertook to keep the covenant, while, in Perry Miller's words, they stood "on the threshold of an inconceivable age."[43]

41. Kerr, "The Character," 113.
42. Hatch, *Sacred,* 181–82; Stout, *New England Soul,* 4–5.
43. Perry Miller, "The Insecurity of Nature: Being the Dudlian Lecture for the Academic Year 1952–1953, Harvard University," 38.

Part II

~※~

THE

INCONCEIVABLE

AGE

INTRODUCTION TO PART II

The ministers of New England, being mostly Congregationalists, are from that circumstance, in a professional way, more attached and habituated to the principles of liberty than if they had spiritual superiors to lord it over them, and were in hopes of possessing, in their turn, through the gift of government, the seat of power. They oppose arbitrary rule in civil concerns from the love of freedom, as well as from a desire of guarding against its introduction into religious matters. The patriots, for years back, have availed themselves greatly of their assistance. Two sermons have been preached annually for a length of time, the one on general election-day, the last Wednesday in May, when the new general court have been used to meet, according to the charter, and elect counsellors for the ensuing year.; the other, some little while after, on the artillery election-day, when the officers are reelected, or new officers chosen. On these occasions political subjects are deemed very proper; but it is expected that they be treated in a decent, serious, and instructive manner. The general election preacher has been elected alternately by the council and the House of Assembly. The sermon is styled the Election Sermon, and is printed. Every representative has a copy for himself, and generally one or more for the minister or ministers of his town. As the patriots have prevailed, the preachers of each sermon have been jealous friends of liberty; and the passages most adapted to promote the spread and love of it have been selected and circulated far and wide by means of newspapers, and read with avidity and a degree of veneration on account of the preacher and his election to the service of the day. Commendations, both public and private, have not been wanting to help on the design. Thus, by their labors in the pulpit, and by furnishing the prints with occasional essays, the ministers have forwarded and strengthened, and that not a little, the opposition to the exercise of that parliamentary claim of right to bind colonies in all cases whatever.

William Gordon

Even though Massachusetts Congregationalist ministers had a long tradition of political preaching and commentary, the American Revolution required an attention to political theory they had never known. From the Stamp Act to the Boston Port Bill, from the battles of Lexington and Concord to the surrender at Yorktown, from the Declaration of Independence to the contests to ratify the constitutions of Massachusetts and the United States, Congregationalist ministers were presented with the enormous task of guiding their parishioners through the establishment of a nation. This required them to set aside the familiar role of defending a commonly accepted constitutional vision and to participate in the task of constitutional creation—a role for which they had not been educated. As Clinton Rossiter reflects,

> The work of the clergy as leaders of political thought was equally impressive. Had ministers been the only spokesmen of the rebellion, had Jefferson, the Adamses, and Otis never appeared in print, the political thought of the Revolution would have followed almost exactly the same line—with perhaps a little more mention of God, but certainly no less of John Locke. In the sermons of the patriot ministers, who were responsible for one fifth to one fourth of the total output of political thought in this decade, we find expressed every possible refinement of the reigning political faith.[1]

In Part II we will examine the Massachusetts Congregationalist clergy's political writing of the founding era. Chronology provides a useful frame for our study. Chapter 4 examines the political theory of the sermons preached prior to the Stamp Act, chapter 5 the political theory of 1764–1776, and chapter 6 Congregationalist political thought from 1777 to 1790. Each chapter also examines important historical events of the period, the textual sources of the documents, as well as the intellectual influences.

1. Rossiter, *Seedtime,* 328.

4

THE APEX OF ENGLISH
CONSTITUTIONALISM
1760–1763

This important Day then, of the annual Exercise of the peculiar Rights of the Inhabitants of this province, by which Rights our civil Polity approaches nearer to that of the happy Island from whence we originated, than that of any other of the British Plantations, and if so, to this Standard of a perfect Government; This joyful Day I say, is most properly opened, by this solemn Act of public Worship; by a devout Address to the Fountain of Wisdom, from whom are derived all the Streams of it, which are dispersed in innumerable human Minds; and by a decent Attention to which, is indeed in the last Resort, the hearkening unto GOD.

Thomas Barnard

In his 1763 election sermon given on the eve of the Stamp Act, Thomas Barnard summarized the Massachusetts Congregationalist clergy's attitude toward England and the future of the province.

> Now commences the Æra of our quiet Enjoyment of those Liberties, which our Fathers purchased with the Toil of their whole Lives, their Treasure, their Blood. . . . Here shall our indulgent Mother, who has most generously rescued and protected us, be served and honoured by growing Numbers, with all Duty, Love, and Gratitude, till Time shall be no more. Here shall be a perennial Source of her Strength and Riches. Here shall Arts and Sciences, the Companions of Tranquility, flourish. Here shall her new Subjects and their Posterity, bless the Day, when their imagined Enemies Victories proved to them the Beginning of the most valuable Freedom. Here shall dwell uncorrupted Faith, the pure Worship of GOD in its primitive Simplicity, unawed, uninterrupted; here shall it extend itself and its benign Influences among those who have hitherto "sat in Darkness, in the Region and under the Shadow of Death."[1]

1. Thomas Barnard, *A Sermon Preached Before His Excellency Francis Bernard Esq. . . .* , 44–45.

Barnard was not alone in his high regard for England and its constitution; during these four years the clergy was effusive with its praise. On the eve of the Stamp Act, the Congregationalists appeared confident that the English Constitution was the most reasonable design for politics.

This chapter examines the political thought of the published occasional sermons preached by Massachusetts Congregationalists from 1760 to 1763. These sermons represent the culmination and maturation of eighteenth-century Congregationalist political thought prior to the founding era. During this period the ministers did not break new ground as much as they stated with more vigor and confidence the political thought that emerged after the establishment of the second charter.

The Congregationalists and the English Constitution

As chapter 2 explained, the English Constitution provided a concept of politics that fit the intellectual needs of Congregationalists. The clergy commended the English Constitution throughout the eighteenth century, but as the revolutionary era approached, ministers were more confident than ever that it constituted the model for colonial politics. The sermons of 1760–1763 are alike in their praise of the English Constitution, and coming off the defeat of the French, the colonial attitude toward Britain was never better. Benjamin Stevens reflected this in his 1761 election sermon: "But to bring our views near home, in this Province;— We are blessed with a constitution formed upon the model of the British Government:—A constitution, which if kept inviolate, will secure to us the blessings of civil society, and the advantages of religious liberty."[2]

Although the ministers were loyal supporters of the English Constitution, in fact they only partially embraced it. This is reflected in their political discourse. They are concerned almost exclusively with three areas: liberty, popular sovereignty, and virtue.

As Nathan Hatch points out, the first love of the Congregationalist clergy was liberty. Therefore it is not surprising that the most important aspect of the English Constitution for the clergy was its defense of religious and civil liberty, and of the two, religious liberty was most important.

Like the Puritans, the Congregationalists believed religious liberty was one of the most important foundations for free government. Stevens expressed the typical view:

2. Benjamin Stevens, *A Sermon Preached at Boston, Before the Great and General Court or Assembly . . . ,* 58–59.

> The connection between religion and liberty is apparent. . . . Religion being the only solid basis of this inestimable blessing, your first regard is due thereto. Religion, indeed, is the first and principal concern of every man, as the favor of his maker, and his happiness in time and through eternity depend upon it. No other principle will so effectually secure the rectitude of your conduct, and lead you with equal uniformity and ardor to seek the welfare of this people.[3]

It is important to note that what the Congregationalists meant by *liberty* differed from what it meant for the Puritans. For both it meant, in some fashion, the freedom of individual conscience in matters of religious belief. The Puritans recognized that faith could and should not be coerced. Both groups also believed that religious liberty had a communal dimension as well—the freedom of the community to serve God as it corporately determined, with individuals expected to conform or leave the community. By the 1760s, however, the corporate importance of religious liberty had showed signs of erosion. The community no longer held the power it once did. Religious liberty had come to mean an individual's right to public toleration of his Protestant denominational choice. Although not explicitly stated, it was assumed that toleration did not extend to atheists or non-Protestants.[4] Nevertheless, even this much toleration, which exceeded what had been realized in England and would have been anathema to the Puritan fathers, was now one of the most cherished components of Congregationalist political thought. As Stevens expressed it,

> Once more, it may be premised, that altho' christianity was properly established by GOD himself or his son Christ Jesus. . . . And although this kingdom was founded when the power of the civil magistrate was armed for it's destruction:—yet should the civil authority think it necessary, as they have in almost all christian countries, to establish any particular form of christianity, let it be considered that all such establishments are evidently human; and unless there be a general toleration, are inconsistent with religious liberty.[5]

Religious liberty, rather than being only the freedom of a sect to form a holy "Citty upon a Hill," was now also understood to be the limited freedom of individual religious conscience and was classified as one of many individual liberties. This is not to say that the corporate dimension

3. Stevens, *A Sermon*, 60.
4. Thomas Barnard, *A Sermon Preached Before His Excellency*, 37.
5. Stevens, *A Sermon*, 10–11.

of liberty had been lost. Barry Shain's assertion that *liberty* had a communal definition during the founding era is certainly correct when applied to Congregationalists.[6] The ongoing importance of the covenant testifies to a strong corporate commitment. Nevertheless, religious individualism had begun to manifest itself during this time.

The clergy's discussion of religious liberty and the English Constitution illustrates a point raised in chapter 2 concerning the difference between the English Constitution and what the clergy attributed to it. The clergy praised the English Constitution for its fierce protection of religious liberty, but the ministers held a conception of religious liberty that surpassed what the English Constitution actually granted at the time. Although this discrepancy does not discount the importance of the English Constitution to the ministers, it does demonstrate that the ministers were not wholly dependent on it for their political theory.[7]

As for civil liberty, the Congregationalists also developed a more individualistic understanding of the concept than did the Puritans. The Congregationalists, drawing on Whig political thought, argued that civil liberty, although not fully defined, was understood to be the variety of rights granted by God to individuals in the state of nature. "As in a *State of Nature prior to Government,* every Man has a Right to the Fruits of his own Labour, to defend it from others, to recover it when unjustly taken away, or an Equivalent, and to a Recompence for the Damage and Trouble caused by this unrighteous Seizure; and to take reasonable Precautions for Security against future Rapine."[8]

Although the Puritans would not have disagreed with these rights, they would not have accepted the individualism that accompanies "state-of-nature" and "rights" language. For the Puritans, liberty was granted by God through membership and participation in a just and holy community of saints. Christian community lay at the heart of Puritan political thought; individual claims would never be upheld against the common good, nor would individuals be allowed to reflect on the possession of liberties independent of their responsibility to the common good and God. The Congregationalists, however, viewed politics in more temporal terms, with government seen as a less holy, though not less important, activity.

6. Shain, *Myth,* 4.
7. F. W. Maitland, *The Constitutional History of England: A Course of Lectures Delivered,* 514–24.
8. Abraham Williams, *An Election Sermon [1762],* 7.

The End and Design of Government, is to secure Men from all Injustice, Violence and Rapine, that they may enjoy their Rights and Properties; all the Advantages of Society, and peaceably practice Godliness:—that the Unjust and Rapacious may be restrained, the ill Effects of their Wickedness be prevented, the secular Welfare of all be secured and promoted.

The Nature of civil Society or Governments is a temporal worldly Constitution, formed upon worldly Motives, to answer valuable worldly Purposes. The Constitution, Laws and Sanctions of civil Society respect this World, and are therefore essentially distinct and different from the *Kingdom of Christ*, which is *not of this World*.[9]

The Congregationalists, in keeping with the English Constitution, established a more individualistic notion of liberty than did the Puritans. They continued, however, the Puritan tradition of emphasizing the relationship between liberty and virtue. Contrary to the more modern notions of liberty, the ministers were keen on educating their parishioners in the relationship between responsibility and rights. The Congregationalists would never have given the individual the right to commit an immoral act, no matter what the circumstances. Individuals were understood as always having the right to act virtuously, but never the right to behave unvirtuously.

After praising religious and civil liberties, the clergy viewed the principle of popular sovereignty as the second most important aspect of the English Constitution. So strongly did the ministers embrace the principle that they opposed the right of a monarch to rule without consent. Using an argument similar to that employed by Thomas Paine, they condemned any suggestion that monarchy is biblically required. Even though they insisted they were grateful to be ruled by a king, they asserted that the English Constitution based the rule of monarchy on the principle of popular sovereignty. According to Thomas Barnard, the Bible "shews how high we may trace the Claim and Practice of civil Societies, to elect such to Places of Trust for the common Benefit, as would in the general Opinion well answer the Ends of their Appointment." Indeed, Abraham Williams echoed other eighteenth-century ministers by arguing that "the *Voice of the People* . . . is the *Voice of God.*"[10]

This is another example of the clergy interpreting the English Constitution in a manner at odds with its mid-eighteenth-century meaning.

9. Ibid.
10. Thomas Paine, *Common Sense*, 71–76; Thomas Barnard, *A Sermon Preached Before His Excellency*, 12; and Williams, *Election Sermon*, 15.

No English constitutional lawyer of this era would have allowed this interpretation. According to F. W. Maitland, sovereignty in this era rested either with the king, the king and Parliament, or the law, but not the people.[11]

It is important to note, however, that although the ministers believed in popular sovereignty, they were neither democrats nor Levellers. Authority rested with the people in a corporate sense, and though all individuals possessed rights, not all were eligible for citizenship. Williams's election sermon provides a fine example of Congregationalist thinking on this point. In it he clearly asserted that all citizens were equal in their natural rights. He argued that in the state of nature, "all men [are] naturally equal, as descended from a common Parent, enbued with like Faculties and Propensities, having originally equal Rights and Properties, *the Earth being given to Children of Men* in general, without any *difference, distinction, natural Preheminence,* or *Dominion* of one over another." Consequently, a government was obligated to protect the rights of all people residing within its boundaries.[12]

Even though humans were equal in rights, not all were capable of ruling or even participating in the responsibilities of citizenship. The Congregationalists had a hierarchical vision of society and believed in a chain of command. All citizens were to be obedient and deferential to the popularly elected government, act responsibly in accordance with their stations, and give attention to the cultivation of their souls. Once again, Williams expressed this well:

> As in the natural Body, the several Members have their distinct Offices, for which they are adapted, and when in their proper Order, they perform their natural Functions, the Body is in it's most perfect State; so in the politic Body, when it's several Orders attend to their respective Duties, proper to their Rank; the Welfare of the whole Community, and of every Individual, is secured and promoted. . . .'Tis the Concern of every Person, in every Station, to attend to his proper Duty, and mind his own Business, if he would be a good Member of Society and promote the public Weal. . . .
>
> Finally, let us all of every Rank and Order, consider our selves as Members of the civil Body, who have our proper Sphere of Action; and whatever Part Providence has assign'd us, let us perform it well. It is not our Concern, who fills this or that Station provided the Duties of it are faithfully performed, and *there be no Schism in the Body.* If the public

---

11. Maitland, *Constitutional History,* 281–301.
12. Williams, *Election Sermon,* 5; see also Stevens, *A Sermon,* 13–14.

> Good be promoted, we ought to be content, tho' we may imagine *our selves,* or some of our Friends, better qualified for some Posts, than the present Possessors.

Citizens and rulers were equal in natural rights but not in ability or social standing.[13] The demands of popular sovereignty were met by the political participation of citizens in the selection of a government that was attentive to the rights of all.

Though popular sovereignty was the primary procedural and structural element of the English Constitution emphasized by the ministers, they also noted the importance of mixed government and the rule of law, which were seen as important in preserving the liberties of the people and preventing tyranny.

> Let us gratefully acknowledge the Goodness of divine Providence, in favouring us with so wise and good a civil Government. A Constitution the best proportioned and adapted to answer the Ends of civil Society, to secure the Enjoyment of our private Properties, and every Satisfaction and Advantage of social Life. By a happy Mixture and Union of the several Forms of Government; most of the Inconveniences of each are avoided, and the peculiar Advantages of each secured.—A Government, so prudently and righteously administered, that most of our Laws are just and reasonable; and in general, equitably executed.[14]

The third element of Congregationalist political thought from 1760–1763 was the importance the ministers attached to virtue for both rulers and citizens. Although the ministers continually attributed this notion to the English Constitution, their conception is unique and appears to be drawn from the Puritans and the Whigs. In keeping with the sermons of the first half of the eighteenth century, ministers were keenly concerned about those who governed them. Indeed, their overall lack of attention to structural details may be due to a belief that the character of a ruler is the most important element in any government. Benjamin Stevens argues that if the rulers are virtuous,

> such a state, whatever was its form of government, must be free. Even in absolute monarchies, if the sovereign is influenced by the spirit of Christ and his religion, without any checks to his power, or fundamental laws or compact to regulate his conduct, he will make the supreme law

---

13. Williams, *Election Sermon,* 10, 17, 5.
14. Ibid., 12; see also Thomas Foxcroft, *Grateful Reflexions on the Signal Appearances of Divine Providence for Great Britain and its Colonies in America, which Diffuse a General Joy,* 9.

of all governments the *safety and happiness of the people,* and not arbitrary will, his rule.[15]

For ministers, especially Jason Haven, the first standard of a good ruler is that he know and love God.

> He, like the author of our religion, whose spirit dwells within him, will rule the people in meekness, and judge in equity. His gentleness will melt those, whom rigour could not subdue. The authority of the ruler, accompanied with the kindness of the christian, will force a willing submission from all; and insensibly learn the rebellious the language of obedience; "what wilt thou have me do?" In consequence of inward serenity, "a law of kindness will dwell upon his lips;" which will often have a more powerful influence and refractory, than the greatest severities of language; and give occasion to say; "how forcible are the right words?" The magistrate will be feared;—the man will be loved;—order will be maintained; and civil government made to answer the excellent ends for which it is designed. Such rulers will be likely "to rule for God, and be faithful; they will be a terror to evil doers, and a praise to them that do well."[16]

The second standard, after religious devotion, is that the ruler have sufficient character, ability, education, and experience for the task. Thomas Barnard exhorts his listeners to choose "such as have in private Life manifested, that the benevolent Affections have powerful Influence upon them, who have conducted worthily in more contracted Spheres of Action."[17] They should also select those who use their minds to

> the amassing civil and political Knowledge; the gaining just Ideas of the general Rights of Mankind natural and social; of the Laws of Nature and Nations; the municipal Constitutions of his own Country; the Genius and Interests of his People; their Connections with, or Dangers from their Neighbours; the Methods of best encreasing their Numbers, Wealth and Extent; the Laws which will render their Liberties more equal and secure; their internal Policy more firm; encourage 'their Trade and Manufactures; promote Virtue and a Spirit of Religion.[18]

Benjamin Stevens asserts that rulers ought to be men who consider posterity, maintain "their own independence, [and] are free from the tyranny of ambition, avarice and other lusts." Samuel Dunbar adds to this

15. Stevens, *A Sermon,* 51.
16. Jason Haven, *A Sermon Preached To the Ancient and Honorable Artillery Company . . . ,* 17–18.
17. Thomas Barnard, *A Sermon Preached Before His Excellency,* 13.
18. Ibid., 25.

by saying that rulers need not only know the laws of the land, but possess the "wisdom, fidelity and courage, to make a right and just application of them."[19]

Ministers were also concerned with the behavior and character of citizens. Although the sermons have very little to say about citizens directly, we can deduce their intentions from what they ask rulers to promote. Quite simply, rulers were to do everything possible to create in citizens the virtue and piety necessary to enjoy liberty responsibly. Benjamin Stevens repeated a theme employed in virtually every eighteenth-century election sermon.

> As fathers of the people, whose duty it is to attend to the interest of the whole family; the children and youth demand your attention: a due regard is therefore to be paid to their education, early to form their minds to knowledge, piety, virtue, industry, and a love of liberty.—May not some farther provision be made, more effectually to promote these ends?[20]

Inculcating piety and virtue was not regarded by ministers or magistrates to be an easy task and, as we have seen, is the one area where the assistance of the church was regarded to be critical. Magistrates were called to lead the state by personal example, through the enforcement of an acceptable moral code, and by doing everything possible to complement the efforts of the church in moral education.

Although policy advocacy is more characteristic of sermons later in the founding era, some discussion of governmental roles is contained in these earlier sermons, with most of it relating to the promotion of virtue. Abraham Williams's election sermon is typical in this regard. He asked the government to "preserve the public from Damage,—to promote social Virtue, Peace and Happiness: To this End they ought to encourage social Worship,—Instructions in Righteousness,—well regulated Schools and Means of Education."[21]

Not all policy advocacy, however, was related to morals. Anticipating a theme prevalent later in the founding era, Benjamin Stevens asked governors to pay attention to the economy.

> One thing more permit me to hint at.—Our situation and circumstances demand a particular attention to our husbandry and trade, . . .

19. Stevens, *A Sermon*, 68; Samuel Dunbar, *The Presence of God with his People, their only Safety and Happiness*, 30.

20. Stevens, *A Sermon*, 64.

21. Williams, *Election Sermon*, 15–16.

> as it is by our improvement of the advantages that result from those
> sources of wealth, our independence is to be maintain'd: May not some-
> thing further be done for their advancement and encouragement—as
> well as to discountence idleness and extravagence, vices that pave the
> way to slavery?[22]

The lack of additional policy advocacy or attention to constitutional
principles and structures is probably a result of the political security of
this time. Clearly, the ministers and their parishioners were comfortable
with political life and did not believe there was a need to reexamine their
basic political assumptions.

Reason, Revelation, Religion, and Politics

As chapter 2 established, the clergy spoke with relative unanimity when it
came to politics, despite the various doctrinal differences within Massachusetts Congregationalism during this era. Nevertheless, a proper
interpretation of the political sermons requires that one doctrinal difference be examined in some detail. The disagreement is epistemological,
and it constitutes the foundational difference between the Old Lights
and the New Lights.

The Old and New Lights were united on the importance of religion for
life and the harmony of reason and revelation. Religion constituted the
foundation of their thought. Like the Puritans, the Old and New Lights
asserted that the purpose of human life was the worship of God. Thomas
Balch made this point explicit in his 1763 artillery election sermon.

> [God] is ever present with all his Creatures, and . . . even the most
> inconsiderable of them are not excepted out of his Dominion and
> Government. It is the Duty of reasonable Creatures to live under a due
> Sense of this Providence. Nor is it enough that we retain the general
> Notion and Belief of it in our Minds, but should take Care to apply
> it to particular Events. For if God knows and orders every Thing that
> happens to ourselves and others, to Nations and Kingdoms, it must be
> the Duty of his People to acknowledge him in all.[23]

The Old and New Lights also agreed on the harmony of reason and
revelation. Both saw themselves as carrying on the rational defense of
the truth embraced by the Puritans.

---

22. Stevens, *A Sermon,* 65–66.
23. Thomas Balch, *A Sermon Preached to the Ancient and Honorable Artillery
Company . . .* , 28.

They disagreed, however, on the potential of unaided human reason to guide human life. The Old Lights were optimistic about the wide-ranging ability of reason to find moral truth, whereas the New Lights were not. Employing a psychology influenced by the Scottish Enlightenment, the Old Lights shifted from a strict Calvinist view of human depravity to an understanding of human nature as composed of tendencies toward good or evil that can be controlled by reason. Thomas Barnard summarized the Old Light position:

> Observation of human Nature fully proves, that the Wisdom of the Creator has made Part of our Frame, two Setts of Affections to impell us to Action, the selfish and the benevolent; in the Ballance of which, the due Proportion of their Influence, the perfect Character in social Life consists. And altho' such is the Influence of Matter, in the different Combination of its Parts, upon Mind; so manifold are the Trials which the same Wisdom sees best for different Creatures; that these Affections, these inward Motives, have very different Proportions in the Make of different Persons; yet by the due Exercise of the Powers of the Mind they may be respectively cultivated or restrained, so as that any one by prudent Conduct in indulging or limiting them, may become entitled to Respect and Love, and promise fair to be a public Blessing.[24]

The theological implications of this difference were important. Whereas the New Lights held a Calvinist position and viewed humans as wholly depraved and completely dependent on God's grace for redemption and sanctification, the Old Lights continued to hold to the necessity of grace for salvation but wavered on the issue of sanctification. Because they believed that the will was composed of competing affections, and that the mind transcended the will, they asserted that natural philosophy was more valuable for life than the New Lights would grant.

This disagreement was potentially divisive, but such a schism did not develop. This may be due to the fact that, although they disagreed about what reason taught, they both championed reason. Living in accordance with reason was just as important to the New Lights as to the Old Lights. Since politics was primarily an affair of reason, they had common ground. Like their Puritan fathers, both Old and New Lights believed the Bible was mostly silent about politics and that reason was a legitimate tool in the creation of government. Hence, when Old Lights like Thomas Barnard or Abraham Williams spoke about politics and common sense, they

---

24. Thomas Barnard, *A Sermon Preached Before His Excellency*, 14.

had common ground with the New Lights, despite their epistemological differences. As Williams states:

> In a wise civil Constitution, all the Orders and Offices, tend by different Ways to the same Point, the public Good; the Way to this, in general, is *plain* and *easy,* to those that will *attend,* and are disposed to walk in it. . . .
> The Nature and End of Government is not so mysterious, but a Person of *common Sense,* with *tolerable Application,* may attain a competent Knowledge thereof, and with an *upright* Heart, *Honourably perform any Part* Providence may assign him.[25]

A second factor connecting the Old and New Lights was their shared view that religion was essential to a virtuous society. Though they may have disagreed concerning the ability of natural reason to discover the contours of morality and virtue, they agreed that religion played an essential role in human behavior. Even if reason could explain how humans should behave, it seemed to lack the ability to create the "upright heart" and motivate people to act accordingly. Religion, however, in its ability to make people fear God, provided the motivation that politics and the state lacked. The New Lights did not agree with his psychology, but they did agree with Abraham Williams's politics:

> Civil Societies have a Right, it is their Duty, to encourage and maintain social public Worship of the Deity, and Instructions in Righteousness; for without *social Vertues, Societies can't subsist;* and *these Vertues can't be expected, or depended on,* without a belief in, and regard to, the Supreme Being, and a future World: Consequently, a religious *Fear* and Regard to God, ought to be encouraged in every society, and with this View, publick social Worship and Instructions in social Virtues, maintained.[26]

Religion—and by religion they almost certainly meant Christianity—continued to have political importance because it was the best inculcator of public virtue. Consequently, the good society required its presence. Benjamin Stevens made this clear in his 1761 election sermon. "As civil authority extends to the good of the community in all respects, it must extend to religion; piety and vertue being connected with the good of civil societies as well as individuals."[27]

Although the members of the clergy were in agreement concerning the importance of religion to politics, they were ambiguous about the

25. Williams, *Election Sermon,* 14.
26. Ibid., 6–7, 8.
27. Stevens, *A Sermon,* 10.

proper relation between church and state. At points, virtually all of the ministers sounded like liberals. They praised reason, celebrated toleration, emphasized the efficacy of moral education, described the state in temporal terms, and appeared to privatize religion. Abraham Williams exemplified this:

> The End and Design of civil Society and Government, from this View of it's Origin, must be to secure the Rights and Properties of it's Members, and promote their Welfare; or in the Apostle's words, *that Men may lead quiet and peaceable Lives in Godliness and Honesty,* (I Tim. 2.1.) i.e. that they may be secure in the Enjoyment of all their Rights and Properties righteously acquired, and their honest Industry quietly proffess it's proper Rewards, and they enjoy all the Conveniences of a social Life, to which Uprightness entitles them; and that Men may peaceably practice Godliness,—may worship & serve the Supreme Being, in the Way they believe most acceptable to him, provided they behave peaceably, and transgress not the Rules of Righteousness in their Behaviour towards others.[28]

If these passages were examined in isolation, it would appear that the Enlightenment had triumphed. The logic of the sermons seems headed in the direction of disestablishment, especially as the ministers condemn the British government's policy on religious toleration. Yet at other points, usually in the same sermon, the ministers preach like the true sons of Puritans. Congregationalism is acknowledged as the established religion and they do not see any need for change. Moreover, they continually emphasize the covenant and the importance of religion in inculcating the virtue necessary for a good nation.

Some of this tension resulted from an attempt on the part of both sides to establish a new synthesis between Old Light reason and revelation, but most of it was inherited. The Congregationalists and their predecessors had been laboring since the second charter to find a way to establish a relationship between church and state that harmonized their vision of religious freedom and their conviction that Christianity was an essential part of a healthy society.

Tension was rooted in the relationship between religion, politics, and virtue. Because of the covenant, a virtuous republic was as important to the Congregationalists as it was to the Puritans. During the Puritan era, church and state had separate but complementary roles in promoting virtue. The state was to encourage virtue and punish vice, but morality was

---

28. Williams, *Election Sermon*, 6–7.

recognized to be a spiritual issue and the church and state must work in tandem to promote the piety and spiritual formation on which true virtue depended. Although church and state had separate roles, a solid working relationship was possible due to their being constitutionally linked. The state had the power of ecclesiastical oversight, and only church members possessed the franchise.

Under the second charter the rules changed. The visible saints no longer had a monopoly on politics, and the state was given a more religiously neutral mission. The success of the new arrangement depended more upon the voluntary spiritual disposition of a wider number of citizens, none of whom were necessarily Christian. If citizens demanded that the state enforce Christian morality, it could, but if they did not, no constitutional mechanism could overrule them. In short, the second charter put in place what could be described as a more liberal constitution. The preamble, however, had stayed the same. The Congregationalists were just as keen as the Puritans to maintain a community virtuous enough to keep the covenant. During this period, the ministers appear uncomfortable with the arrangement, but they do not acknowledge that any constitutional problems exist. They are comfortable with Congregationalist dominance, are committed to its continuance, and persist in defending the arrangement.

The Sources of the Sermons

As we have seen, the political thought exhibited in the sermons of this period differs significantly from that of the Puritans. The sermons of 1760–1763 illustrate the new ideas, sources, and principles of biblical interpretation the ministers employed in making this shift. Although the Congregationalists' emphasis on virtue is consistent with that of the Puritans, a significant change has occurred in other areas.

The sermons reflect a familiarity with Whig political thought and the Scottish Enlightenment, and a knowledge of the great political thinkers of antiquity. The degree to which classical thought affects these sermons appears minimal. Classical citations surface regularly but are used for illustrative purposes rather than substance. Among the citations found in the sermons are the *Apologue* of Menerius Agrippa, several references to the Athenian republic, references to Pompey, Caesar, and Alexander, as well as to many other anonymous ancient citations.[29]

---

29. Thomas Barnard, *A Sermon Preached Before His Excellency,* 9–10; Stevens, *A Sermon,* 66; Jason Haven, *A Sermon Preached To,* 13.

The impact of Scottish Enlightenment and Whig political thought on Congregationalists is more substantial, as indicated by the clergy's use of Scottish Enlightenment psychology and the "English Constitution." The documented and undocumented references and allusions employed in the sermons dramatically underscore their debt.

Abraham Williams was clearly familiar with state-of-nature theory, though he cites none of it. Benjamin Stevens utilized long quotations from Burlemaqui on civil liberty, Francis Hutcheson on moral philosophy, and Bishop Butler on liberty. Stevens also referred to Philip Doddridge's interpretation of Galileo and Seneca, Lohrman's dissertation on Hebrew government, and Thomas Newton's scholarship on antiquity.[30] The erudition of the Congregationalists and their dedication to reason is evident throughout their sermons.

Given the impact of various Enlightened ideas on the political thinking of the ministers, a new biblical interpretation was required to support it. As they reexamined the Old Testament, they concurred with their predecessors that although the Puritans were correct in their quest for liberty, they were mistaken in their understanding of the best constitutional means to achieve it.

Whereas the Puritans drew their political theology from the story of Israel during the theocracy of Moses, the Congregationalists found biblical justification for their political theory in the story of Israel under the Davidic monarchy. For example, the text of Samuel Dunbar's 1760 election sermon is 2 Chronicles 15:1–2, focusing on King Asa.[31]

A further illustration of the clergy's use of Scripture at this time can be seen in Benjamin Stevens's election sermon. In it he made an elaborate defense of the Congregationalist conception of liberty. Beginning with the Exodus, he reexamined biblical history only to find

> that in the execution of the grand plan before-mentioned, heaven appears in a most signal manner to rescue a particular people from a state of the most miserable tyranny and servitude. The whole history of that important event, the deliverance of Israel from their Egyptian bondage, shews in the strongest manner, God's tender compassion for the rights of his people, and that he will sooner or later appear to take vengeance on the tyrants and cruel oppresors of mankind. The noblest eloquence, inspired by the warmest spirit of liberty, could not use stronger expressions than are found in the sacred writers when they touch upon this subject.[32]

30. Stevens, *A Sermon.*
31. Dunbar, *The Presence*, 1; see also Stout, *New England Soul*, 166–81, 293.
32. Stevens, *A Sermon*, 13.

Sounding a theme that anticipates twentieth-century liberation theology, Stevens argued that the history of God's dealing with humanity was the history of God rescuing his people from bondage and providing the political means to enjoy liberty. He condemned the "Babylonian, Persian, Grecian, and Roman Empires, as they were all tyrannical and oppressive monarchies."[33]

Stevens found that the New Testament supported this post-Puritan vision of liberty, because it demonstrated God's continued effort, through the work of Christ, to establish a just polity that separates "Religion and civil government" and grants the full range of religious and civil liberties to its citizens.[34] The New Testament from Matthew to Revelation shows God's ongoing commitment to this scheme.

Although Stevens was quick to remind his listeners that no polity could claim divine sanction, he argued that the English Constitution best realized the liberating message of Scripture.

> We have long had the happiness of enjoying a most excellent con-
> stitution of government: A government in which the prerogative of the
> sovereign and the privledges of the people are so tempered, that they
> mutually support one another—"A constitution formed on common
> reason, common consent, and common good: A constitution of free
> and equal laws, secured against arbitrary will, and popular licence, by
> an admirable temperament of the governing powers, controling and
> controled by one another". The English constitution is not only the
> pride of Britons, but the envy of its neighbors.[35]

The Congregationalists found not only that reason and Scripture supported their embrace of England and its constitution, but also, so did an examination of God's providential work in history. Thomas Foxcroft's 1760 thanksgiving sermon, reflecting the enthusiasm that accompanied the defeat of France, presented a comprehensive and dramatic reinterpretation of the history of New England. Foxcroft's reading of providential history was at many points diametrically opposed to that of the Puritans. The Puritans were careful to keep Massachusetts and England separate, regarding England as the great temptress and potential corruptor of the "errand in the wilderness." Foxcroft, however, saw that God bound England and New England together and destined them for great things.

33. Ibid., 23.
34. Ibid., 32.
35. Ibid., 56.

And surely, upon the least Reflexion, all must confess, the merciful
Favours of Providence towards us (I mean the People of *Great Britain,*
and of these its dependent Colonies) have been both *great* and *manifold;*
and if view'd in a proper Light, must be own'd the worthy Subject
of our devout Meditation, and just Matter of our joyful and solemn
Thanksgiving to God. . . . If we should . . . recollect the great *Deliver-
ances* . . . which God has wrought for us in Times of Distress; the great
Preservations he has granted us in Times of Danger; and the great *positive
Blessings,* Liberties, Privileges, and Advantages, Successes, Increases,
Improvements, Extent of Dominion and Commerce, Superiority in
War, intestine Tranquillity, Health, Wealth, Plenty, a well-ballanced Con-
stitution of civil Government, salutary Laws, and innumerable other
Instances of national Glory and Bliss, by which God has signaliz'd his
Goodness and Bounty towards us; it would, on the whole, be abundantly
manifest, that *the Lord hath done great Things for us:* and indeed, *hath not
dealt so with any Nation* besides on the Face of the Earth.[36]

Although the clergy of this period was committed to popular sovereignty, its members regarded the reigning English monarch as legitimate
and worthy of respect. Foxcroft's sermon illustrates this in his reinterpretation of royal history. He speaks well of the reign of Edward VI,
and, in a move that demonstrates the remarkable shift that occurred in
Congregationalist thought since the previous century, praises Elizabeth I
for her purification of religion and attention to liberty, while completely
ignoring the reign of Cromwell. This interpretation of English history
directly contradicts that of the Puritans. They viewed Queen Elizabeth
with disdain, "for she did not purify the church of its ceremonies and
vestments," and saw Cromwell as a heroic politician of great courage and
vision.[37]

Foxcroft condemns Charles I because of his attack on liberty, property,
Parliament, and the Church, and denounces Charles II on a similar score.
The climax of Foxcroft's revision is the coronation of William and Mary,
which is depicted as the turning point of British history. "This was an Event
fruitful of abundant Happiness and Glory to the Nation: particularly, in
the Establishment of *civil Liberty,* and Provision for the Security of the
Protestant Religion, by a Parliamentary Settlement of the *Succession* to the
Crown."[38]

Just sixty-nine years earlier, Congregationalists were upset with William
over the terms of the second charter; a century earlier the ascension of

36. Foxcroft, *Grateful Reflexions,* 8–9.
37. Morgan, *Puritan Dilemma,* 19.
38. Foxcroft, *Grateful Reflexions,* 18.

Cromwell was seen as a sign of God's realization of the reform of England. Yet now, William is celebrated, the reign of Cromwell is ignored, and religious liberty is understood in terms of toleration.

By 1763, England and its constitution appeared to have won the affection of the Congregationalists. Over the course of the next decade, however, the ministers would find it necessary to reexamine their affection and find out how much of their thought was British, and how much of it their own.

5

BUILDING A NEW CONSTITUTION
1764–1776

F̵rom what has been said in this discourse, it will appear that we are in the way of our duty in opposing the tyranny of Great Britain; for . . . there cannot remain a doubt in any man, that will calmly attend to reason, whether we have a right to resist and oppose the arbitrary measures of the King and Parliament; for it is plain to demonstration, nay, it is in a manner self-evident, that they have been and are endeavoring to deprive us not only of the privileges of Englishmen, and our charter rights, but they have endeavored to deprive us of what is much more sacred, viz., the privileges of men and Christians, i.e., they are robbing us of the inalienable rights that the God of nature has given us as men and rational beings, and has confirmed to us in his written word. . . . We have made our appeal to Heaven, and we cannot doubt but that the Judge of all the earth will do right.

Samuel West, 1776

In early 1764, Massachusetts Congregationalists had every reason to be optimistic about the future. The French had been defeated, there was peace with England, and it seemed to many that the millennium was at hand.[1]

The Sugar Act of 1764 and the Stamp Act of 1765 initiated a chain of events that confounded this vision, demanding that ministers respond to the disintegration of British-American relations. Although the Congregationalists did not lose their millennial hope, they discovered that the English Constitution was no longer viable. A different constitution was required, and 1764–1776 was the period of its construction.

The attachment of the ministers to England was not easily broken. Like so many of the colonists, they regarded revolution as unthinkable

---

1. Ruth H. Bloch, *Visionary Republic: Millennial Themes in American Thought, 1756–1800,* xi–50; Hatch, *Sacred,* 21–54 passim.

until late in 1774. Initially they resisted revolution but later embraced it wholeheartedly. The sermons that best illustrate this transformation are the election sermons that stand on either side of this era: Andrew Eliot's of 1765, and Samuel West's of 1776.[2] By comparing and contrasting these sermons, the shift that occurs in Congregationalist political thought during this period can be illuminated.

Andrew Eliot's 1765 Election Sermon

The Sugar and Stamp Acts precipitated the crisis that led to the Revolution, but the ministers, like others, were not quick to recognize it. Unfortunately, the clergy's reaction to the Sugar Act is unknown. Due to a smallpox epidemic, no election sermon was given in 1764, and the only published occasional sermon of the year was given by Edward Barnard before word of the act reached the colonies.[3] Andrew Eliot's 1765 election sermon, published two months after passage of the Stamp Act and the only published occasional sermon of 1765, provides insight into the clergy's reaction to a colony in uproar.

Eliot's response was measured. On the whole, his sermon resembled the sermons of 1760–1763 by reaffirming the basic tenets of eighteenth-century Congregationalist political thought. Indeed, Bernard Bailyn finds it to be the prototypical pre-revolutionary Congregationalist sermon.

> Eliot's purpose in addressing the assembled magistrates on the occasion of the annual election was not to probe or extend the received tradition but to transmit it intact, with only the most modest embellishments. In structure the sermon could scarcely have been a more rigid embodiment of the inherited formulas: discussion, first, following presentation of the Biblical text, of "the character of a good ruler"; second, of "the duty of subjects to their rulers." . . .
> . . . Its chief importance lies in precisely that fact: in its fine articulation of a tradition of thought familiar to every New Englander, if not to every American, exemplifying at the outset of the Revolutionary era the substratum of belief that underlay the developing rebellion.[4]

2. It should be noted that there were two Massachusetts Congregationalist ministers of this period named Samuel West. This Samuel West graduated from Harvard in 1754 and ministered in New Bedford. The other Samuel West graduated from Harvard in 1761 and pastored in Needham and Boston. For clarity's sake, when the other Samuel West is discussed his name will be followed by (Needham).

3. Edward Barnard, *A Sermon Preach'd April 12, 1764 on the Public Fast. . . .*

4. Bernard Bailyn, "Religion and Revolution: Three Biographical Studies," 96, 97.

Eliot's sermon was true to well-established Congregationalist protocol. It opened with a section of biblical exposition that provided a summary of eighteenth-century Congregationalist political theology. Eliot used both the Old and New Testaments to argue that although God had intentions for political life, Scripture provided only the contours, leaving reason to work out the details. "Reason we say dictates that there should be government; and the voice of reason is the voice of God. But what form of government they will be under is left to the choice of those who are to be governed. God has never determin'd this."[5]

The innovative aspect of his biblical exposition lay in his emphasis on the republican and consensual nature of Hebrew politics under the Judges, rather than the Davidic mixed monarchy on which the clergy had focused throughout the century.

> According to the original constitution of the Hebrew polity, "each tribe was under it's own proper and distinct government; and order'd it's affairs by it's own princes, heads of families, elders and courts". At the same time, there was a union of all the tribes, the whole congregation had a right to meet together, either personally or by their representatives, to consult the common good and the prosperity of the whole. (5)

This interpretation had important implications for Massachusetts Congregationalist political thought because of the way it enabled the ministers to shift their attention from England and the monarchy to a republican vision of self-government. As Harry Stout points out, Eliot's interpretation foreshadows what will become the standard mode of biblical interpretation by the time of the Revolution.

> In a very real sense, the Old Testament had always served as New England's "ancient constitution," and each generation had read and interpreted it from their own unique vantage point. The first two generations focused on the "theocracy" of direct divine rule; the third and fourth on "Israel's Constitution" in its anglicized, "mixed" form under the Davidic dynasty. In 1775 New England's embattled ministers again returned to the Old Testament, but this time their attention was riveted on the premonarchic period of the "Jewish Republic."[6]

In terms of New Testament hermeneutics, Eliot continued the practice of interpreting the teachings of Christ and the apostles to mean that

5. Andrew Eliot, *A Sermon Preached Before His Excellency Francis Bernard, Esq. . . . ,* 17. Subsequent references to this sermon will appear in this chapter as page references only.
6. Stout, *New England Soul,* 293.

Christians ought to submit to those rulers placed over them, provided
they governed in accordance with Christian liberty. He recognized the
difficulty in discerning the line between submission and resistance, but he
did not believe that the thirteenth chapter of Romans required unlimited
submission (41–44).

With this biblical basis, Eliot launched into a discussion of the political principles that reason provides. He argued that "the necessity of
government arises wholly from the disadvantages, which, in the present
imperfect state of human nature, would be the natural consequence of
unlimited freedom." All government was formed by the "compact and
mutual consent" of the citizens, and "it is the undoubted right of the
community to say who will govern them; and to make what limitations or
conditions they think proper" (8, 17, 18).

Eliot asserted that "there are certain constitutions, which are the basis
and foundation of the state, and which are obligatory on those who govern, as well as those who are governed" (19). Like the ministers who pre-
ceded him, Eliot was a fierce defender of these liberties or "constitutions"
but did not define them. He clearly believed in the rights of compact and
consent, as well as conscience. Individual religious liberty continued to
be important, but beyond compact, consent, and conscience, Eliot was
not precise.

Despite the fact that Eliot laid out a biblical rationale for self-government and asserted that Britain had violated the fundamental liberties of
the colonists, he unapologetically defended the English Constitution and
affirmed the monarchy.

> In GREAT BRITAIN there is a happy mixture of monarchy, aristocracy,
> and democracy. This is perhaps the most perfect form of civil govern-
> ment. It is the glory of Britons and the envy of foreigners. . . .
>   It is the safety of the British nation that it's monarchy is hereditary,
> as that right is now understood. It is a favor of heaven, that our lawful
> Sovereign is posses'd of virtues, which ensure him the love and obedi-
> ence of his subjects. (18, 48)

Eliot did acknowledge the present unrest but offered a measured response, passing off the crisis as a misunderstanding.

> Such a critical season, if I mistake not, is the present and I cannot easily
> be mistaken, when all orders of men are so generally alarmed, in this
> and the other colonies, and apprehend their most valuable privileges
> in danger.
>   I am far from impeaching the justice of the British Parliament. If any
> acts have pass'd that seem hard on the colonies, we ought to suppose,

they are not owing to any design formed against them, but to mistakes and misrepresentations. (51–52)

Eliot reflected the early reaction of the clergy to the conflict with England, in that even in the midst of turmoil, he defended the English Constitution as the best form of government. He expressed appreciation for both the monarchy and Parliament, using Burlemaqui and Montesquieu to support his argument. Like Abraham Williams, he did not believe that every man is fit to govern or that citizens can always be trusted to elect the best magistrates. Eliot was suspicious of the electoral process because of the possibility that political campaigns might encourage charlatans to seek office and discourage people of merit. Consequently, he praised constitutional monarchy for the way it reduced this danger by not giving citizens too much freedom in appointing their rulers (16, 39–40). He did not, however, offer further explanation or elaboration of the English Constitution's components or merits.

The truest indication that Eliot's sermon was consistent with those preceding it is found in his extended discussion of the character of a good ruler. Eliot argued in the major part of his sermon that the most important single component of good government was a good ruler.

> Rulers cannot come up to the character of the text, unless they are men of religion and virtue. Every condition has its temptations, none are exposed to more or greater, than those who are advanced to stations of power and eminence; none have greater need of a settled principle of action, and the assistance of divine grace. If there is no regard to God or the rules of virtue, wisdom degenerates into cunning, and rulers instead of endeavouring to know what Israel ought to do, only consider what they have to do themselves; instead of aiming at the public good, they consult only what is like to promote their own private interest, support their administration, and continue them in power. . . . Vice contracts the mind, and quenches every spark of public spirit; it fills the soul with criminal prejudices, and the higher it is exalted, the mischief is so much the more extensive. (23–24)
>
> In addition to moral virtue, a ruler should possess a good degree of wisdom and knowlege—That they are particularly acquainted with the constitution of the country they are called to govern. . . . And that they have prudence to conduct affairs in seasons that are critical and alarming. (10)

Moreover, Eliot was not afraid to share some wisdom with the ruler, advising him to proceed with caution when levying taxes, to watch out for neighbors who may encroach, and to consult the good of distant generations when evaluating the implication of every measure (14–16).

Eliot made clear, however, that of all the ruler's duties, none were more important than the responsibility to promote religion and virtue among the citizens. Just as it is essential that men of virtue and piety be selected as magistrates, so must citizens grow in their own knowledge and practice of true religion and virtue. For Eliot, the chief problem facing Massachusetts was not the Stamp Act, but its own iniquity. Such an assertion was fully in step with the Puritan and Congregationalist commitment to keeping God's covenant with Massachusetts. Eliot was confident that if the citizens of Massachusetts exhibited piety and virtue, God would grant prosperity to them. In a passage reminiscent of Increase Mather railing on the moral condition of Massachusetts in 1679, Eliot argued:

> he must have but little understanding of the times, who does not see that we are in more danger from our internal vices, than from any external impositions. Our luxury, extravagance and intemperance threaten our ruin. We live above ourselves, we have forsaken the simplicity of our fathers in our dress, our furniture and our tables. We import much that is absolutely superfluous, that tends only to feed our pride and vanity. (55)

He went on to review the problem of alcoholism in Massachusetts and discuss the study of Dr. Stephen Hales on the danger of presenting alcohol to children aged five and under (56).

Although Eliot stood firmly for toleration and the freedom of conscience in religious matters, he believed that due to the public moral benefits of Christianity, rulers must promote the outward observance of its laws and moral teachings:

> There is one course, which if it will not be a certain cure, will yet be a great relief in the most dangerous state we can be in; and that is the practice of piety and universal virtue. Virtue does in itself tend to promote public happiness. Frugality, temperance, industry will extricate us out of most difficulties that can arise; and if we are actuated by religion, God will be our God, our protector, and friend; "it will be well with us and our children for ever." Whatever he does else, if a ruler has understanding in the times, he will promote the fear of God and obedience to his laws. (35)

Eliot's use of sources is also typical of the preceding decade. Reflecting a familiarity with the political climate of his day, his sermon was influenced by classical and Whig sources. Indeed, Eliot cites Burlemaqui, Montesquieu, Livy, and Horace.

Gradually Realizing Revolution

Unfortunately, Eliot's sermon was the only published occasional sermon of 1765, so discerning whether other clergy responded to the Stamp Act in such a measured way is not possible. On August 25, 1765, Jonathan Mayhew preached an unpublished sermon relating to the Stamp Act, and in so doing, incited a riot that resulted in the destruction of Governor Hutchinson's home.[7] Mayhew, however, apparently backed away from the radical implications of that sermon in his 1766 thanksgiving sermon, *The Snare Broken.*

The sermon is somewhat vague and allows both patriots and Tories to find comfort. Trevor Colbourn emphasizes its revolutionary nature by pointing to Mayhew's defense of colonial rights on which neither Parliament nor the Crown may ever infringe.[8] Conversely, Bernard Bailyn points out that Mayhew was in line with Eliot by endorsing the authority of England, the English Constitution, and condemning the riots

> which had so recently and grievously been associated with his name, and to disassociate any such action from his well-known libertarian views that he devotes the central passages of the sermon. Political freedom, he writes, . . . is in no way a natural progenitor of civil upheaval. Its natural complement is not defiance but obedience to constituted authority, to King, Parliament, and the laws of Britain's free constitution. Parliament's right to superintend the colonies, "to direct, check, or control them," is universally conceded "whatever we may think of the particular right of taxation," . . . .[9]

Despite Mayhew's ambiguity, Nathaniel Appleton's 1766 thanksgiving sermon unequivocally supported the monarch, the Parliament, and the constitution:

> All that I have further to add here is, that in our praises and thanksgivings to God for this present merciful deliverance, we join our humble fervent prayers that this our tranquility may be lengthened out to future generations . . . . And indeed considering, how fully this affair was debated in parliament, and the judgment of some eminently learned in the law, of both houses of parliament relative to constitutional right, and taking many other things into consideration, we have no ground to fear any thing of this sort, so long as we approve ourselves loyal subjects

7. Bailyn, "Religion and Revolution," 114.
8. Colbourn, *The Lamp,* 63–65.
9. Bailyn, "Religion and Revolution," 123.

of king George, and his successors in the British throne; and yield all due subjection to the British Parliament.[10]

While other ministers may have expressed their opposition to the Stamp Act more forcefully than did Appleton, at its heart Appleton's sermon appears to be a good measure of the ongoing support the clergy had for England and the constitution.

As the decade progressed, however, the relationship between England and the colonies became strained and the ministers began to distance themselves politically from Britain. Sermons in the latter half of the 1760s emphasized commitment to the English Constitution but are conspicuous in that they no longer expressed blanket confidence in the monarch and Parliament. Instead, they emphasized the government's intrinsic responsibility to protect citizens' liberty. Daniel Shute expressed this sentiment in his 1768 election sermon.

> A compact for civil government in any community implies the stipulation of certain rules of government. These rules or laws more properly make the civil constitution. How various these rules are in different nations is not the present enquiry; but that they ought in every nation to coincide with the moral fitness of things, by which alone the natural rights of mankind can be secured, and their happiness promoted, is very certain. And such are the laws of the constitution of civil government that we, and all *British* subjects are so happy as to live under.[11]

The Boston Massacre of March 5, 1770, was the watershed event of this era. While ministers still longed for reconciliation with Britain, their sermons became more self-righteous and defiant in tone. The moral fitness of Britain to rule was called into question, and the possibility of revolution began to be raised. Stout writes:

> In a rare (though not unprecedented) departure from usual custom, Boston's ministers interrupted the regular sermon series on the first Sunday following the massacre to comment directly on the shootings. From his Old North pulpit, John Lathrop thundered forth God's condemnation. . . . If Britain did not change its policy of government by force and violence, it did not deserve to rule: "That *government* which, rejecting the foundation of *law,* would establish itself by the *sword,* the sooner it falls to the ground the better." Nor, Lathrop concluded, could any doubt the righteousness of resistance to such a government: "If

10. Nathaniel Appleton, *A Thanksgiving Sermon on the Total Repeal of the Stamp-Act,* 29–30.
11. Daniel Shute, *An Election Sermon [1768],* 117.

the essential parts of any system of civil government are found to be inconsistent with the general good, the end of government requires that such bad systems should be demolished, and a new one formed, by which the public weal shall be more effectually secured."[12]

Other ministers, such as Ebenezer Gay, refrained from invoking revolutionary imagery but agreed with the sentiment by equating British occupation of Boston with the Babylonian captivity.[13] He, along with other ministers, called on the people to repent so they might be released from this great oppression that had overtaken them.

Despite the horror of the massacre, the ministers still affirmed England and its constitution but became more explicit and selective about what they were affirming. No longer was the English Constitution viewed in vague and almost mystical terms; rather, the ministers rapidly developed a more precise understanding of the nature of good government. As A. W. Plumstead argues, Samuel Cooke's election sermon of 1770 symbolized this shift.

> Cooke's sermon has few Biblical quotations and references; it is more disinterested, more philosophical than the earlier Biblical sermons. It blends a presentation of ideas because they come from God with a presentation of ideas because they are true and reasonable in themselves. Many of the principles on which the Declaration of Independence rests are already here: Civil government is an ordinance of God; only the people have the right to choose who will rule them; government must contain a balance of power with built-in checks (a subject he returns to for special emphasis); people have a "right" to good government; a ruler will not forget that his subjects are "by nature equal" to himself; the people will be subjected to no restrictions not founded on reason; laws must be clear and explicit; the constitution of a government must not be supported by a standing army (as with the present King's directives to Massachusetts); freedom of speech is a "right inherent in the people." Although he hopes for a reconciliation of the differences with Britain, his review of colonial history . . . is clear in intent; America has a right to enjoy and direct her own domain—a right sanctioned not only by God (the chosen people motif takes on new political meaning), but now by almost one hundred and fifty years of history.[14]

During the next seven years the ministers, as well as their compatriots, grew more precise and confident in their constitutional demands. Upon

12. Stout, *New England Soul,* 272–73.
13. Ebenezer Gay, *The Devotions of God's People Adjusted to the Dispensations of His Providence.*
14. Plumstead, *The Wall,* 324–25.

receiving no favorable response from Britain, they did not back down but preached resistance, even armed resistance. In 1771, Eli Forbes preached the annual election sermon for the Ancient and Honorable Artillery Company. He emphasized the dignity and importance of the military character, as well as the necessity of Christian citizens to prepare to defend themselves and their liberties.[15] Elisha Fish applied this teaching specifically to Massachusetts in his sermon entitled *The Art of War Lawful, and Necessary for a Christian People.* In the foreword, written in 1774, Fish explains his purpose in printing this sermon.

> It is now submitted to the publick Eye, with his earnest Wish and Prayer, that it may serve the Purpose designed, by exciting the young Men to whom it was first delivered, in their commendable Exercises, and stir up others to the like Exercises; and be also an Occasion of moving some more able Pen to spread this martial Fire through our happy Land.[16]

A proliferation of published sermons indicates that 1774 was a year of revolutionary significance for the Congregationalists. Of the seventy sermons published between 1764 and 1776, half came out between 1774 and 1776. By 1774 the sense of doubt raised by the Boston Massacre had grown significantly. Congregationalists were sensing that reconciliation might be hopeless, and there was talk of nationalism and revolution. In December 1774 Isaac Story was the first Massachusetts Congregationalist of this period to refer to the citizens of Massachusetts as "Americans" in a published sermon,[17] and William Gordon joined the numbers of Congregationalists who were asking what citizens of Massachusetts should do if they could not be reconciled with Great Britain.

> The important day is now arrived, that must de[ter]mine whether we shall *remain* free; or, alas! be brought into bondage, after having long enjoyed the sweets of liberty. The event will probably be such as is our own conduct. . . .
> Will we make our appeal to heaven against the intended oppression; venture all, upon the noble principles that brought the house of *Hanover,* into the possession of the *British* diadem; and not fear to bleed freely in the cause, not of a particular people, but of mankind in general; we shall be likely to transmit to future generations, though the country should be wasted by the sword, the most essential part of the fair patrimony received from our brave and hardy progenitors, the

15. Eli Forbes, *The Dignity and Importance of the Military Character Illustrated.*
16. Elisha Fish, *The Art of War Lawful and Necessary for a Christian People . . . ,* 2.
17. Isaac Story, *The Love of our Country Recommended and Enforced,* 17.

right of possessing, and of disposing of, at our own option, the honest fruits of our industry?[18]

Oliver Noble in March 1775 answered the question affirmatively, confidently proclaiming that "the Cause of AMERICA . . . is the cause of GOD, never did Man struggle in a greater, or more glorious CAUSE."[19]

By 1776 the Revolution had begun, and the ministers were firmly in support. They now had a clear and deep sense of the constitutional liberties and privileges to which they were entitled. Since Britain refused to act honorably, they saw revolution as the only course open to a Christian people. Peter Whitney, making great use of the Declaration of Independence, summed up the attitude of the ministers.

> The necessity therefore, we have been under, of throwing off our connection with Great-Britain, renouncing king George, and his evil counsellors, and setting up as independent states, plainly appears. We could get no relief: if we had submitted to their usurped jurisdiction, we must have been in a state of the most abject slavery and wretchedness; and because we *could* not submit, we are threatened to be devoured with the sword. We have not been rash and hasty in declaring ourselves independent; as the ten tribes were in their revolt from Rehoboam; but we have waited even unto long suffering. These thirteen years have we been suffering from the cruel hands of tyrants, and merciless oppressors; "in every stage of these oppressions we have petitioned," entreated, *cried* for relief, but they have made their hearts as an adamant stone, that they might not hear us. When such a long train of abuses, and usurpations, pursuing invariably the same object evinces a design to reduce us under absolute despotism, it is our right, it is our duty to throw off such government, and provide new guards for our future security.[20]

Whitney's sermon illustrates the change in Congregationalist political thought that had taken place since Eliot's election sermon, and Samuel West's election sermon of 1776 reveals the depth and nature of the change.

Samuel West's Election Sermon of 1776

Samuel West's sermon is similar in form to Eliot's. The sermon employed the same outline and themes: an opening section of biblical exposition

18. William Gordon, *A Discourse Preached December 15th, 1774 . . .* , 11–12.
19. Oliver Noble, *Some Strictures Upon the Sacred Story Recorded in the Book of Esther . . .* , 20.
20. Peter Whitney, *American Independence Vindicated*, 29–30.

that discussed foundational and theoretical elements, a description of the character of a good ruler, and a conclusion stressing the ruler's duties. What differs is the theory and emphasis. Constitutional structure and political theory were somewhat undeveloped before this period, but they now take on new prominence. West and the other ministers, forced by circumstances to reconsider their relationship to England and the English Constitution, developed a new and more detailed political theory.

West began his sermon with biblical exposition and political theology. In a familiar reading of the New Testament, he argued that Christ and the apostles do not endorse any specific form of government. Moreover, obedience is only owed to magistrates who govern for the public good.[21] Like his predecessors, West also asserted that Christian revelation yields the same conclusions as reason. The Bible, "being rescued from the absurd interpretations which the favorers of arbitrary government have put upon it, turns out to be a noble confirmation of that free and generous plan of government which the law of nature and reason points out to us" (430). West supported the legitimacy of this interpretation in Old Light fashion by defending the priority of reason and natural law over revelation. In doing so he employed an argument reminiscent of that exhibited by Locke in his *Letter Concerning Toleration.* "A revelation, pretending to be from God, that contradicts any part of natural law, ought immediately to be rejected as an imposture; for the Deity cannot make a law contrary to the law of nature without acting contrary to himself,—a thing in the strictest sense impossible" (414).

Having established the importance of reason, West quickly moved away from an explication of Scripture to a rational exploration of human nature. Like Abraham Williams, he anchored his discussion in the Scottish Enlightenment. In contrast to the Puritans, who embraced a Calvinist vision of human depravity, West asserted that men are by nature social creatures interested in seeking the public good. West contended, like David Hume and Francis Hutcheson,

> that we may be the more firmly engaged to promote each other's welfare, the Deity has endowed us with tender and social affections, with generous and benevolent principles: hence the pain that we feel in seeing an object of distress; hence the satisfaction that arises in

21. Samuel West, *On the Right to Rebel Against Governors,* 423–32. Subsequent references to this sermon will appear in this chapter as page references only.

relieving the afflictions, and the superior pleasure which we experience in communicating happiness to the miserable. (411)

West then laid out a political theology heavily influenced by social contract theory. To do so, West used a logic of discourse reminiscent of Sidney and Locke.

> The Deity has . . . invested us with moral powers and faculties, by which we are enabled to discern the difference between right and wrong, truth and falsehood, good and evil: hence the approbation of mind that arises upon doing a good action, and the remorse of conscience which we experience when we counteract the moral sense and do that which is evil. This proves that, in what is commonly called a state of nature, we are the subjects of the divine law and government; that the Deity is our supreme magistrate, who has written his law in our hearts, and will reward or punish us according as we obey or disobey his commands. (411)

West depicted a state of nature that, "though it be a state of perfect freedom, yet is very far from a state of licentiousness. The law of nature gives men no right to do anything that is immoral, or contrary to the will of God" (413–14). According to West, the state of nature is also a state of equality. What set West's conception apart from his contemporaries' was the extent of equality. He asserted that many, if not most, of the differences between men were attributable not to nature but to education.

> The great difference that we may observe among several classes of mankind arises chiefly from their education and their laws: hence men become virtuous or vicious, good commonwealthsmen or the contrary, generous, noble, and courageous, or base, mean-spirited, and cowardly, according to the impression that they have received from the government that they are under, together with their education and the methods that have been practised by their leaders to form their minds early in life. (432)

In spite of his high view of reason, West did not believe that humans would live responsibly in the state of nature. Due to the degenerate state of the human race, the law of nature did not have sufficient rational force to persuade fallen human beings to live in peace:

> The law of nature is a perfect standard and measure of action for beings that persevere in a state of moral rectitude; but the case is far different with us, who are in a fallen and degenerate estate. We have a law in our members which is continually warring against the law of the mind, by which we often become enslaved to the basest lusts, and are brought into bondage to the vilest passions. The strong propensities of our animal nature often overcome the sober dictates

of reason and conscience, and betray us into actions injurious to the public and destructive of the safety and happiness of society. (415)

As a consequence, men in the state of nature: form themselves into politic bodies, that they may enact laws for the public safety, and appoint particular penalties for the violation of their laws, and invest a suitable number of persons with authority to put in execution and enforce the laws of the state, in order that wicked men may be restrained from doing mischief to their fellow-creatures, that the injured may have their rights restored to them, that the virtuous may be encouraged in doing good, and that every member of society may be protected and secured in the peaceable, quiet possession and enjoyment of all those liberties and privileges which the Deity has bestowed upon him; *i.e.,* that he may safely enjoy and pursue whatever he chooses, that is consistent with the public good. This shows that the end and design of civil government cannot be to deprive men of their liberty or take away their freedom; but, on the contrary, the true design of civil government is to protect men in the enjoyment of liberty. (415–16)

As in earlier Congregationalist thought, an ideal form of government was not stipulated: "The modes of administration may be very different, and the forms of government may vary from each other in different ages and nations; but, under every form, the end of civil government is the same, and cannot vary: it is like the laws of the Medes and the Persians—it altereth not" (416).

Unlike earlier sermons, however, West in this sermon articulated a detailed and coherent account of the political condition of any just society: what a government owes its citizens, and what citizens owe a government. To begin with, government must be based on the consent of the governed. "All the members of a community have a natural right to assemble themselves together, and act and vote for such regulations as they judge are necessary for the good of the whole." In addition, when

a community is become very numerous, it is very difficult, and in many cases impossible, for all to meet together to regulate the affairs of the state; hence comes the necessity of appointing delegates to represent the people in a general assembly. And this ought to be looked upon as a sacred and inalienable right, of which a people cannot justly divest themselves. (419)

West further argued that because representatives are to reflect the will of the people, the deliberative meeting place must not be geographically distant from the people, such as in a foreign land (419).

Majority rule should govern the political decision making of the society, whether through the assembly of the people or their representatives:

> It is also necessary that the minor part should submit to the major;
> *e.g.,* when legislators have enacted a set of laws which are highly ap-
> proved by a large majority of the community as tending to promote the
> public good, in this case, if a small number of persons are so unhappy
> as to view the matter in a very different point of light from the public,
> though they have an undoubted right to show the reasons of their
> dissent from the judgment of the public . . . it is the duty of those few
> that dissent peaceably and for conscience's sake to submit to the public
> judgment. (418)

As long as rulers were qualified and governed competently and mor-
ally, the people owed them support and loyalty:

> While . . . they rule in the fear of God, and while they promote the
> welfare of the state . . . it is the indispensable duty of all to submit to
> them, and to oppose a turbulent, factious, and libertine spirit, whenever
> and wherever it discovers itself. When a people have by their free
> consent conferred upon a number of men a power to rule and govern
> them, they are bound to obey them. Hence disobedience becomes a
> breach of faith; it is violating a constitution of their own appointing,
> and breaking a compact for which they ought to have the most sacred
> regard. (417)

Thus West was careful to emphasize the importance of obedience under
normal conditions.

When rulers, however, did not observe and protect the rights of the
people, then revolution, even violent revolution, was justified.

> When a people find themselves cruelly oppressed by the parent state,
> they have an undoubted right to throw off the yoke, and to assert their
> liberty . . . for, in this case, by the law of self-preservation, which is the
> first law of nature, they have not only an undoubted right, but it is
> their indispensable duty, if they cannot be redressed any other way, to
> renounce all submission to the government that has oppressed them,
> and set up an independent state of their own. (419–20)

Using this basis, West evaluated the British government and found,
unlike Eliot, that the undeclared revolution in which the colonists found
themselves was entirely warranted.

> It would be highly criminal not to feel a due resentment against such
> tyrannical monsters. It is an indispensable duty, my brethren, which we
> owe to God and our country, to rouse up and bestir ourselves, and,
> being animated with a noble zeal for the sacred cause of liberty, to
> defend our lives and fortunes, even to the shedding the last drop of
> blood. The love of our country, the tender affection that we have for our
> wives and children, the regard we ought to have for unborn posterity,

yea, everything that is dear and sacred, do now loudly call upon us to use our best endeavors to save our country. (438–39)

Although West focused primarily on these fundamental issues of form, procedure, and legitimacy, he did not ignore the responsibility and character of rulers. He argued that rulers serve to promote the social good by protecting the liberties of all people. This was best accomplished by enacting "good laws to encourage every noble and virtuous sentiment, to suppress vice and immorality, to promote industry, and to punish idleness, that parent of innumerable evils; to promote arts and sciences, and to banish ignorance from among mankind" (432).

The role of the magistrate in promoting virtue and punishing vice, though not emphasized to the same degree as by Eliot, was still important. West argued that although government existed to protect the liberty of citizens, the magistrate needed to punish vice and prevent activity harmful to society. "If we consult our happiness and real good, we can never wish for an unreasonable liberty, viz., a freedom to do evil, which . . . is the only thing that the magistrate is to refrain us from" (430).

Not only should magistrates promote virtue, they must themselves be virtuous. West, however, did not emphasize the importance of a ruler's character to the same degree as did earlier ministers. Whereas earlier sermons emphasized the accountability of the magistrate to God, West and the clergy of his day were more egalitarian, seeing the magistrate as more of a servant. Nevertheless, West still saw a ruler's character as important: "From this account of civil government we learn that the business of magistrates is weighty and important. It requires both wisdom and integrity. When either are wanting, government will be poorly administered; more especially if our governors are men of loose morals and abandonèd principles" (433–34).

More important than the virtue of magistrates was the virtue of citizens. Since religion was still regarded as the surest promoter of good citizenship and societal felicity, the magistrate could do no better than to ensure that the dictates of religion were taught and obeyed: "As nothing tends like religion and the fear of God to make men good members of the commonwealth, it is the duty of magistrates to become the patrons and promoters of religion and piety, and to make suitable laws for the maintaining public worship, and decently supporting the teachers of religion" (432). Although the magistrate should encourage adherence to the outward dictates of religion, he must not violate an individual's liberty of conscience, a sacred right. West went further than many of his fellow clergymen, however, by arguing that the politically favored status of Congregationalism be extended to other religious groups. This was to be done by allowing people to let their parish taxes go to the church of their choice (432–33).

West found his conclusions supported not only by reason and revelation but also by providence. In keeping with the Puritan and Congregationalist emphasis on providential history, West reexamined New England history and argued, like the Massachusetts clergy had for 140 years, that if the people of Massachusetts kept the covenant, victory would be guaranteed.

> Our fathers fled from the rage of prelatical tyranny and persecution, and came into this land in order to enjoy liberty of conscience, and they have increased to a great people. Many have been the interpositions of Divine Providence on our behalf, both in our fathers' days and ours; and, though we are now engaged in a war with Great Britain, yet we have been prospered in a most wonderful manner. And can we think that he who has thus far helped us will give us up into the hands of our enemies? Certainly he that has begun to deliver us will continue to show his mercy toward us, in saving us from the hands of our enemies: he will not forsake us if we do not forsake him. Our cause is so just and good that nothing can prevent our success but only our sins. (440)

Congregationalist Political Thought at the Revolution

As we have seen, prior to the founding era, the Congregationalist clergy celebrated the English Constitution, and in its name developed a political theory based on a variety of Puritan and Enlightened sources. When the challenges of the revolutionary period confronted the ministers, and when it became clear that the English Constitution was no longer suitable, the ministers found they had the resources necessary to forge a political identity and constitution independent of England. Whereas pre-revolutionary ministers had referenced the state of nature before, ministers of this era, such as Samuel West, found in state-of-nature theory a form in which to recast their political theory. While West's political theory is not necessarily inconsistent with earlier eighteenth-century preaching, he has clearly clothed it in a more "enlightened" robe.

West's sermon betrays Old Light unitarian and rationalist leanings to which New Light trinitarians would certainly object. Samuel Langdon, President of Harvard and a trinitarian, condemned such theology in his 1775 election sermon.

> We have rebelled against God. We have lost the true spirit of Christianity, though we retain the outward possession and form of it. We

have neglected and set light by the glorious gospel of our Lord Jesus Christ, and his holy commands and institutions. The worship of many is but mere compliment to the Deity, while their hearts are far from him. By many the gospel is corrupted into a superficial system of moral philosophy, little better than ancient Platonism; and, after all the pretended refinements of moderns in the theory of Christianity, very little of the pure practice of it is to be found among those who once stood foremost in the profession of the gospel.[22]

Nevertheless, despite their theological disagreement, New Lights, including Langdon, were able to endorse West's political theory. For instance, Langdon's 1775 election sermon uses language and comes to conclusions remarkably similar to West's.

By the law of nature, any body of people, destitute of order and government, may form themselves into a civil society, according to their best prudence, and so provide for their common safety and advantage. When one form is found by the majority not to answer the grand purpose in any tolerable degree, they may, by common consent put an end to it, and set up another.[23]

Langdon differs from West in emphasis. Langdon spent an entire half of his sermon addressing the importance of virtue. If there was a political debate among ministers at the close of this period and into the next, it was over the relative importance affixed to constitutional and structural issues, as opposed to moral issues. Both were seen as important but to differing degrees. Langdon accepted West's political theory, but he, like some others, gave more weight to the importance of Massachusetts's moral condition when developing a prognosis of the commonwealth's health.

The 1775 thanksgiving sermon of Samuel Baldwin further illustrates the political unity of the clergy and the wide-ranging use of state-of-nature thinking. Coming from a more rural parish and apparently affiliated with the trinitarian camp, Baldwin employed in his political teaching the same argument employed by West and Langdon.

What are called natural rights, are in part surrendered, whenever mankind voluntarily enter into society and form into bodies-politick;— which surrender, ought ever to be with this express, or at least, tacit view and design—the promoting the greater security and advantage

22. Samuel Langdon, *Government Corrupted by Vice, and Recovered by Righteousness . . .* , 242.

23. Ibid., 250.

of every individual, and the more extensive happiness of the collective body—the sole true end of all government. The rights of conscience are unalienable. . . . Life, liberty and property are an inheritance secured by the immutable laws of nature.[24]

Two phrases in Baldwin's sermon were frequently used in other Congregationalist sermons of this period, though not by Eliot or West. Ministers frequently argued that the purpose of government was to promote, first, the "happiness" of the people, and, second, their "life, liberty, and property." These phrases abound in the sermons of this era and represent the importance of these rights to the ministers. While not using the same language, Eliot and West affirm the same ideas by emphasizing that the central concern of government is the promotion of liberty.

Sources of the Sermons

As before, the Bible was the most referenced source in this period's sermons. The most significant development in biblical interpretation was the clergy's attention to the Jewish republic rather than the Davidic monarchy. Although the clergy's political thinking was primarily based on reason, it was still important that their politics remain consistent with Scripture.

While many sermons lacked any extra-biblical references, they, like most of the sermons of the eighteenth century, demonstrated a familiarity with contemporary political discourse. Since referencing sources was not customary for sermons, a lack of citations does not mean lack of influence or familiarity. The sermons contained many classical references, though their use appears somewhat peripheral. Despite the ministers' classical education, their allusions to classical ideas, references to classical writers, and use of classical quotes were, on the whole, illustrative. Those quoted or referenced during this time included Alexander the Great, Julius Caesar, Aristides, Livy, Cicero, Herodotus, Xenophon, Plutarch, and several anonymous Latin writers.

Sources from the Enlightenment were referenced more frequently and appear to play a larger role in these sermons. Hume, Burlemaqui, Montesquieu, Hoadley, Milton, Trenchard, Hutcheson, Sidney, Pope, and Bacon are all referenced, but by far the most frequent referenced

24. Samuel Baldwin, *A Sermon Preached at Plymouth, December 22, 1775 . . .* , 14, 26.

extra-biblical source during this period was John Locke. William Patten's 1766 sermon is a clear example of the clergy's use of Locke.

> Sentiments very different from these, were entertained by the great Mr. Lock, which he has very clearly expressed, in his essay on government, particularly, Essay 2, chap. 18,19, one paragraph from the latter I shall transcribe. After consulting the doctrine of passive obedience, he proceeds thus: "Here 'tis like, the common question will be made, who shall be judge, whether the prince or legislature act contrary to their trust? This perhaps, ill-affected and factious men may spread among the people, when the prince only makes use of his just prerogative. To this I reply, the people shall be judge; who shall be judge whether his trustee or deputy acts well, and according to the trust reposed in him, but he who deputes him, and must, by having deputed him, have still a power to discard him, when he fails in his trust? If this be reasonable in particular cases of private men, why should it be otherwise in that of the greatest moment, where the welfare of millions is concerned; and also, where the evil, if not prevented, is greater, and the redress very difficult, dear, and dangerous."[25]

This is one of many quotations of Locke employed during the successive decade.

Another major change in the sermons of this period, at which West's sermon only hints, is the latest revision of Puritan and Congregationalist history. At the outset of this period, the Puritan founders were portrayed either as champions of an enlightened notion of religious liberty and the English Constitution, or as an unenlightened people whose true goals were realized in the establishment of religious toleration and the English Constitution in the second charter in 1691. This latter vision is illustrated in Amos Adams's thanksgiving sermon of 1769:

> The views on which this land was settled were singular and noble: It was not trade and commerce, nor any worldly views, but religion was the noble motive that brought our father hither. . . . They were indeed, in general a very serious consciencious set of people. In some things they appear to us, at this day, to have been narrow in their principles, but, if we reflect, we shall find nothing singular in them on that account. The age they lived in was dark, compared with ours. . . . Time and enquiry, experience and observation for more than an hundred years have increased the light, and taught the more sensible part of christians moderation, candor, and forbearance. . . .
> . . . The sacred thirst for liberty brought our fathers hither. They endured the yoke of slavery with great uneasiness. The first hints

25. William Patten, *A Discourse Delivered at Hallifax . . .* , 17.

that William and Mary had ascended the throne, aroused them to spirited measures . . . . After three or four years the present charter was obtained. . . . It's priviledges we wish, and pray may be transmitted a fair inheritance to our children after us.—Only I would observe, that one of our ministers, the Rev. Dr. Increase Mather, was a principal agent in obtaining the present charter. His praise is in all the churches: His name will be remembered thro' many generations.[26]

In Samuel Baldwin's 1775 thanksgiving sermon, the "narrow" Puritan founders were now held up as champions and models of reformed republican government, and at the same time Increase Mather and the second charter were no longer regarded as highlights of providential history.

Our forefathers in the infancy of Plymouth colony, disclaimed all authority of parliament over them, that in their corporate capacity, being legally assembled, did ordain, constitute and enact, that no act, imposition, law or ordinance should be made, or imposed upon them, then, or in time to come, but such as should be made or imposed by consent of the associates or their representatives legally assembled.[27]

As Samuel Baldwin's sermon intimates, a change had occurred in the outlook of the ministers since 1764. At the outset of this period, they possessed an underdeveloped political thought that emphasized liberty, popular sovereignty, and the importance of virtue. By the end of the period the ministers had incorporated these ideas into a more sophisticated political theory. Using this, they justified the Revolution and provided the contours of a new Congregationalist constitution.

What remained for the ministers to resolve was the debate between Langdon and West concerning the place and importance of virtue in a successful polity. In addition, they still needed to apply their constitutional theory to the practical tasks of forming a new commonwealth and nation: tasks that the clergy faced following the Revolution.

26. Amos Adams, *A Concise, Historical View of the Perils, Hardships, Difficulties and Discouragements which have Attended the Planting and Progressive Improvements of New England . . .*, 63–64, 27.

27. Baldwin, *A Sermon Preached*, 25.

6

THE TRIUMPH of VIRTUE?
1777–1790

Virtue is justly represented as the spirit of a republican government. Have we a sufficiency to animate ours? If the spirit be departed the form will be of but little worth. Had the people of these States, in fact, possessed those measures of public and private virtue, which the confederation gave them credit for; that might have proved a foundation for many generations. Experience has given the most unequivocal proofs, that it did not possess energy sufficient for us. And though we promise ourselves much from the National Constitution, so happily effected, organized and commenced, yet we may by no means expect to be happy under it, without our own consent and co-operation too.

If we are not prudent and cautious in our elections to important public offices: If we are impatient of the necessary restraints and expence of good government: If we indulge to mean groundless jealousies and suspicions of those in authority; and give a loose rein to the vices too prevalent in the present day; and especially if we get beyond the restrains of religion, and bid adieu to the fear of God: Have we not every reason to expect, that our most pleasing prospects will be soon closed, and succeeded by the deepest gloom?

Josiah Bridge

By 1777 the Congregationalists had developed the framework of their "new" political theory, but one question remained, and it concerned the role of religion in the commonwealth. Throughout the eighteenth century, religion and virtue had been regarded as essential to a good polity, but the relationship between government and religion was ambiguous. This ambiguity was seen in sermons throughout the founding era. Samuel West's 1776 election sermon placed more emphasis on structures and procedure than on piety and virtue, whereas Samuel Langdon opposed any political theory that devalued the importance of piety and virtue to political life. By 1790, Congregationalists appeared united on their answer. Nevertheless, a lingering doubt remained.

The Congregationalist Constitution

Following the Revolution, three ideas from the earlier eras combined to form the mature Congregationalist constitution: Old Light epistemology, republican political theory, and the covenant. To begin with, the Old Light emphasis on the importance of reason for politics was more pervasive than ever. The 1786 election sermon of Samuel West (Needham) illustrated this:

> Revelation indeed was not essentially necessary to inform mankind, that as civil government ought to be the result of mutual agreement, designed for the good of all; so they who contribute most to the accomplishment of that design, are entitled to its first distinctions. This, like the first principles of science in general, is by the wisdom and goodness of its Author, enstamped on human nature; and like the essentials of religion, is written on the hearts of men, as by the finger of God . . . . The religion of Jesus assumes no other authority over mankind, than what arises from the native excellence of its doctrine and precepts, and the influence which they have on the hearts and lives of men. It is connected with civil society only, as it enriches the heart with every virtue which tends to adorn human nature, and to increase social happiness.[1]

Second, republican thinking pervades the sermons in a multitude of ways. As before, the state of nature forms the basis for theological reflection and political reasoning. Simeon Howard's 1780 election sermon illustrates this: "Suppose, then, a number of men living near together, and maintaining that intercourse which is necessary for the supply of their wants, but without any laws or government established among them by mutual consent, or in what is called a state of nature."[2]

The purpose of government was still understood to be the promotion of the public happiness. The Massachusetts Congregationalist clergy would certainly support Barry Alan Shain's contention that "for Revolutionary Americans, the common or public good enjoyed preeminence over the immediate interests of individuals."[3] For the Congregationalists, the public good was the goal. As Phillips Payson stated: "The voice of reason and the voice of God both teach us that the great object or end of government is the public good."

1. Samuel West (Needham), *A Sermon, Preached Before His Excellency James Bowdoin, Esq.* . . . , 9, 12.
2. Simeon Howard, *A Sermon Preached Before the Honorable House of Representatives of the State of Massachusetts-Bay* . . . , 362.
3. Shain, *Myth*, 3.

The form of government best suited to provide it was republican government. Payson continued: "Nor is there less certainty in determining that a free and righteous government originates from the people, and is under their direction and control; and therefore a free, popular model of government—of the republican kind—may be judged the most friendly to the rights and liberties of the people, and the most conducive to the public welfare."[4]

As Zabdiel Adams pointed out, the ministers believed the best republican government was one framed by a constitution that protected the right of the people to make laws in accordance with the public good through representatives of their own choosing.

> Several things are necessary to procure chearful obedience to laws, besides their being enacted by men in our own election. Particularly, first, they should be agreeable to the *genius* of the people, and the *spirit* of the *constitution*. The *constitution* contains the fundamental principles of the state in which we live. It is the *civil compact* and points out the manner in which we chuse to be governed, the *privileges* of the people, and the *prerogatives* of the governing body. These powers are ceded to others, not for the sake of aggrandizing any class of men; not for the purpose of keeping up the vain distinction among those who by nature are equal; not that *some* may *riot* in *plenty*, whilst *others* are indigent and distressed; but only that they may use them for the public good.[5]

Samuel Webster concurred in his 1777 election sermon: "In the first place, . . . [the magistrate's] duty is (with the assent of the people) to frame the most just and equitable constitution; calculated, in the best manner which human wisdom can devise, to answer the great and only design of government, *the security* of the *lives, liberty* and *property* of the people."[6]

At the outset of this period, the clergy's primary concern was winning the war. Of the six sermons published in 1777, five dealt exclusively with the Revolution and focused on reassuring parishioners of the justness of their cause. William Gordon made this point clear in his sermon preached on the anniversary of the Declaration of Independence to the Massachusetts General Court.

> I heartily congratulate you upon [God's] having brought [the revolution] to pass, as the only secure way for your continuing free. I see

4. Phillips Payson, *A Sermon Preached Before the Honorable Council . . .* , 524.
5. Zabdiel Adams, *A Sermon Preached Before His Excellency John Hancock, Esq. . . . ,* 546–47.
6. Samuel Webster, *A Sermon Preached Before the Council . . .* , 12.

not how it is possible for you to be ever more dependent upon Great-Britain, without being in a state of bondage, and feeling all the horrors of slavery. I have not a doubt but that we are fully authorised by reason and religion for thus seperating; and am persuaded that we are justified by the disinterested and impartial world.[7]

Samuel Webster concurred:

When therefore we see in a manner, the whole world, except these *American States*, groaning under the most abject *slavery*, with so few *successful attempts* to deliver themselves, how *stupid* must we be, if we do not exert ourselves to the utmost to save ourselves from falling into this *remediless* estate, this bottomless gulf of misery.[8]

After victory was assured, the clergy turned their attention to state-craft, and they made scattered recommendations on constitutional issues. Phillips Payson, for instance, advocated the adoption of abbreviated terms of office, separated powers, and checks and balances.

On account of the infinite diversity of opinions and interests, as well as for the other weighty reasons, a government altogether popular, so as to have the decision of cases by assemblies of the body of the people, cannot be thought so eligible; nor yet that a people should delegate their power and authority to one single man, or to one body of men, or indeed, to any hands whatever, excepting for a short term of time. A form of government may be so constructed as to have useful checks in the legislature, and yet capable of acting with union, vigor, and despatch, with a representation equally proportioned, preserving the legislative and executive branches distinct, and the great essentials of liberty be preserved and secured.[9]

Not surprisingly, the ministers were pleased with the terms of the Massachusetts Constitution. Simeon Howard spoke for the group when he stated:

This may also lead us to reflect, with pleasure and gratitude to God, upon the steps which have been taken by this people to frame a new constitution of government, and that a plan has been formed which appears, in general, so well calculated to guard the rights and liberties, and promote the happiness of society, and which, it is to be hoped, will soon be the foundation of our government.[10]

7. William Gordon, *The Separation of the Jewish Tribes . . .* , 28.
8. Webster, *A Sermon*, 26.
9. Payson, *A Sermon*, 524–25.
10. Howard, *A Sermon Preached Before*, 383.

The ministers were more comfortable in offering policy recommendations. Charles Chauncy, in a plea common to this period, asked the government to deal with the problem of inflation and paper currency.

> As the emission of *paper-bills* was necessary to the carrying on the war, they might think a law of this kind would tend to prevent their depreciation, and with this view be determined to make it: But as it is now known, notwithstanding this, and every other device, that the depreciation has been amazingly great, and that hundreds and thousands of helpless widows and orphans, to say nothing of others, have been reduced to the utmost distress by means of it, together with the law that has given it an oppressive efficacy, it may be reasonably expected, that *the powers that now be* will interdict the continuance of this law, lest there should be the continuance of that injustice, which would be a disgrace to even a pagan state.[11]

Among the "others" of whom Chauncy said "nothing" are ministers. Since ministers were frequently paid at a fixed rate, the inflation associated with the war severely devalued their already modest salaries, especially where communities were not inclined to renegotiate their packages. Not surprisingly, ministers frequently expressed their concerns regarding the effects of inflation on widows and orphans and "others" during this period.

The ministers had many other policy concerns. Samuel Webster advocated public support for schools and colleges, keeping the militia well regulated, eliminating standing armies in peacetime, and regulating prohibition of monopolies. Phillips Payson encouraged the general distribution of property and the liberty of the press. Simeon Howard lobbied for equitable taxation, and Zabdiel Adams, first cousin of John Adams, exhorted the government to promote both industry and frugality.[12]

What is unique about these sermons is the growing sense that religious establishment may be inconsistent with the political theory they were defending. Some made such a strong case for individual religious freedom that little place is left for an established religion. Samuel West (Needham) made an eloquent defense of religious freedom in his 1786 election sermon:

> We wish not to see our civil rulers officially interfering in matters of religion. Sacred be the rights of conscience! No law can have religion

11. Charles Chauncy, *The Accursed Thing Must be Taken Away From Among a People, If They Would Reasonably Hope to Stand Before their Enemies*, 18.
12. Webster, *A Sermon*, 29–31; Payson, *A Sermon*, 530; Howard, *A Sermon Preached Before*, 392; and Adams, *A Sermon*, 554–55.

for its subject, without infringing those rights, or laying an improper bias on the minds of men, with respect to the first and most important duty of life, that of judging and acting for themselves in those cases where they can only be answerable at the bar of Jehovah.[13]

The ministers argued so passionately for religious liberty that the logic of their sermons points to disestablishment.

Yet, on the other hand, they could not accept such a conclusion because they were also convinced of religion's importance in the promotion of the virtue necessary for society. Their problem was finding a logical way to defend religious freedom and an established religion, and they did not know how to do it. So although they extolled the importance of individual religious freedom, they made virtually no mention of Congregationalism's established status. Instead they merely reminded the rulers and citizens of the covenant and the importance of piety and virtue to their common future.

In one respect, there was nothing novel in this approach to the problem. It is essentially the same answer the Congregationalists had embraced since the second charter. What was new was the sense of immediacy, passion, and conviction with which they communicated it. While they had always been concerned about piety and virtue, a new urgency appeared during this period. This was expressed in many ways, the first of which was the importance of piety and virtue in the character of a good ruler. Phillips Payson, as so many clergy before him, discussed the requirements of a good ruler.

> The qualities of a good ruler may be estimated from the nature of a free government. Power being a delegation, and all delegated power being in its nature subordinate and limited, hence rulers are but trustees, and government a trust; therefore fidelity is a prime qualification in a ruler; this, joined with good natural and acquired abilities, goes far to complete the character. . . . The greatest restraints, the noblest motives, and the best supports arise from our holy religion. The pious ruler is by far the most likely to promote the public good. His example will have the most happy influence; his public devotions will not only be acts of worship and homage to God, but also a charity to men. Superior to base passions and little resentments, undismayed by danger, not awed by threatenings, he guides the helm in storm and tempest, and is ready, if called in providence, to sacrifice his life for his country's good.[14]

13. West (Needham), *A Sermon, Preached Before His Excellency*, 27.
14. Payson, *A Sermon*, 532–33.

Secondly, it was a requirement of a good society.

> Statesmen may plan and speculate for liberty, but it is religion and morality alone which can establish the principles upon which freedom can securely stand. The only foundation of a free constitution is pure virtue; and if this cannot be inspired into the people at large, in a greater measure than we have reason to think they possess it now, they may change their rulers and the forms of their government, but they will not obtain a lasting liberty; they will only exchange *tyrants* and *tyrannies*.[15]

Rulers are again exhorted to do everything possible to promote virtue. According to Simeon Howard, the ruler

> ought, therefore, to have power to punish all open acts of profaneness and impiety, as tending, by way of example, to destroy that reverence of God which is the only effectual support of moral virtue, and all open acts of vice, as prejudicial to society. He should have power to provide for the institution and support of the public worship of God, and public teachers of religion and virtue, in order to maintain in the minds of the people that reverence of God, and that sense of moral obligation, without which there can be no confidence, no peace or happiness in society.[16]

Religion is so important to politics that without it, as Phillips Payson states, the whole political enterprise is in danger:

> I must not forget to mention religion, both in rulers and people, as of the highest importance to the public. This is the most sacred principle that can dwell in the human breast. It is of the highest importance to men,—the most perfective of the human soul. The truths of the gospel are the most pure, its motives the most noble and animating, and its comforts the most supporting to the mind. The importance of religion to civil society and government is great indeed, as it keeps alive the best sense of moral obligation, a matter of such extensive utility, especially in respect to an oath, which is one of the principal instruments of government. The fear and reverence of God, and the terrors of eternity, are the most powerful restraints upon the minds of men; and hence it is of special importance in a free government, the spirit of which being always friendly to the sacred rights of conscience, it will hold up the gospel as the great rule of faith and practice.[17]

The ministers were so convinced of the importance of religion because they were certain that the success of the nation was dependent upon keeping the covenant. The ministers assured their audiences of God's

---

15. Adams, *A Sermon,* 557.
16. Howard, *A Sermon Preached Before,* 374.
17. Payson, *A Sermon,* 529.

support and strength by reminding them, as Phillips Payson did in 1782, of their status as covenant people and how God was demonstrating his faithfulness to them, even as he had to their fathers.

> The finger of GOD has indeed been so conspicuous in every stage of our glorious struggle, that it seems as if the wonders and miracles performed for Israel of old, were repeated over anew for the American Israel, in our day. The hardness that possessed the heart of Pharaoh of old, seems to have calloussed the heart of the British King; and the madness that drove that antient tyrant and his hosts into the sea, appears to have possessed the British court and councils, and to have driven them and their forces to measures, that, in human view, must terminate in their own confusion and ruin.[18]

Yet not only was God's providence in the past and present proclaimed, but so were his millennial promises for the future. If citizens kept the covenant, not only would they be blessed in accordance with the covenant, they would also experience the glory of the millennium. As Ruth Bloch points out:

> Upon the triumph of American arms and the settlement of peace, American revolutionary millennialism rose to its last fever pitch in the early 1780's. Numerous clergymen who printed sermons celebrating the victory described the Revolution as establishing the basis for the future Kingdom of God. God had secured the American republic in order "to prepare the way for the promised land of the latter days."[19]

Samuel West was one of these clergymen, and in his 1777 Plymouth anniversary sermon, using images reminiscent of Winthrop's "Citty upon a Hill" he invoked a millennial promise:

> From our text and context, we have then the utmost trust in God, that he will yet shew us his salvation, and grant a final victory over our foes; and that upon our obtaining a compleat deliverance from our enemies, and establishing our independence, pure religion will revive and flourish among us in a much greater degree of perfection than ever it has done before: That this Country will become the seat of civil and religious liberty; the place from which christian light and knowledge shall be dispersed to the rest of the world; so that our Zion shall become the delight and the praise of the whole earth, and foreign nations shall suck of the breasts of her consolations, and be satisfied with the abundant light and knowledge of Gospel truth, which they shall derive from her that America shall be the place to which the persecuted in other nations shall flee from the tyranny of their oppressors, where they shall find a

18. Phillips Payson, *A Memorial of Lexington Battle . . .* , 8.
19. Bloch, *Visionary Republic,* 94.

safe retreat, and shall be cherished by her like children by a tender mother: and that peace and quietness shall be established upon a firm and lasting basis.[20]

The ministers also employed the jeremiad. Realizing the millennial vision required keeping God's covenant through collective and individual piety and virtue, and the ministers found a dangerous lack of this in the commonwealth. As Henry Cumings observed, if sin continued to prevail, the Revolution would be for nought.

> And here, let me observe, that nothing darkens our prospects more, or gives us more reason to be fearful, as to the event of the present contest, than the great and general prevalence of unrighteousness among us. He must have been very unobserving, who does not know, that by means of unrighteousness, the body-politic has been, and still is, labouring under a dangerous disease. . . .
>
> The goodness of our cause does not make success certain. A good cause often suffers, and is sometimes lost, by means of sin and folly of those, who are engaged in it. This is a consideration, which ought to lie with weight on our minds, at the present day, and engage us to *put away the evil of our doings*, and *keep ourselves from every wicked thing.*[21]

Cumings was not alone in finding deficiency in the collective virtue. Charles Chauncy argued that the colonists' difficulty in winning the Revolutionary War was due to an evil obsession with wealth.

> It will not, it cannot with any face of reason, be denied, that sin, in every kind, abounds in the land.—But if I may speak what I believe is the real truth, I would say, *that sin* which is the source of every other sin, and may emphatically be called the ACCURSED THING AMONG US, is *sordid avarice*, an *unsatiable thirst for money.* . . . And in this view of our character, as having reigning in us *this avaricious disposition*, which has been, and is still productive of all wickedness, what can we expect but the frowns of heaven upon our military operations?[22]

The solution? Piety and virtue.

> And God will deal, in general, after the same manner, with other people, as he dealt with his *Israel*. While they walk with him, and do that which is right and just and good, he will make their enemies to be at peace with them, or deliver them into their hands: But if they violate

20. Samuel West, *An Anniversary Sermon Preached at Plymouth, December 22d, 1777. . . . ;* see also Charles Turner, *Due Glory to be Given to God*, 29.

21. Henry Cumings, *A Sermon Preached at Lexington . . .* , 677.

22. Charles Chauncy, *The Accursed Thing*, 23–24.

the law of God, and *trespass in the accursed thing*, he will not enable them to stand before their enemies, but will give them into their hands.[23]

If the colonists are righteous, they can be assured of God's intervention and the establishment of America, the New Israel; if not, they can be assured of failure and destruction.[24]

Reason may illuminate the constitution and laws of the best polity, but the ultimate success of Massachusetts required that the covenant be kept by a religious and virtuous citizenry. Although they were uncomfortable with established religion, they were unwilling to argue for disestablishment. Establishment was their contingency plan in the event virtue faltered. They were convinced that politics was not a self-sufficient enterprise, and that it needed religion to succeed. The clergymen were uncomfortable in requiring its presence, but given the importance of keeping the covenant, they found it necessary to do so.

So pervasive is this message that, of the twenty-nine sermons published from 1777 to 1783, twenty-two remind the listeners of the covenant and call them to piety and virtue. In their annual election sermons, ministers gave advice on a whole array of policy and constitutional issues but emphasized piety and virtue as the most important factors for winning the war and succeeding as a nation.

The sermons in the second half of this period, from 1784 to 1790, are fully in line with the direction and ideas expressed in those of the first part. The only significant difference is the declining attention given to constitutional and structural issues. This can be attributed to the ministers' satisfaction with the Massachusetts Constitution and relative satisfaction with the condition of the national government. Although ministers mention of the Articles of Confederation and the Constitution, they do so in exclusively favorable terms. Joseph Lyman, Josiah Bridge, and Thomas Barnard all endorse the state and national constitution, with Barnard best summarizing their perspective.

> Our national Government strengthens this conception of our situation. The more thoroughly and impartially we contemplate this plan of government, the more fully we shall be persuaded it is well calculated to promote our publick and private safety and felicity. To give us justice, order, and peace at home, and growing reputation abroad—To lessen the danger of internal dissension and foreign war, and put in action all the causes of national honour and prosperity.—It secures us all our

23. Ibid., 14–15.
24. John Lathrop, *A Discourse Preached on March the Fifth, 1778*, 16–20.

rights, as men and christians: And has within itself the strong principles of wise self-regulation.[25]

In regard to sources, the Bible continued to be the most quoted book, and not surprisingly, the Jewish republic continued to be the textual focus of this period's sermons. The use of the Davidic monarchy as a normative example for politics was dead.[26] It is perhaps surprising that virtually no classical or Enlightenment sources were quoted by ministers after 1776. Samuel Cooper offered an explanation:

> Neither does the time allow, nor circumstances require, that I should enter into a detail of all the principles and arguments upon which the right of our present establishment is grounded. They are known to all the world; they are to be found in the immortal writings of *Sidney* and *Locke,* and other glorious defenders of the liberties of human nature; they are also to be found, not dishonored, in the acts and publications of America on this great occasion, which have the approbation and applause of the wise and impartial among mankind, and even in Britain itself: They are the principles upon which her own government and her own revolution under William the third were founded; principles which brutal force may oppose, but which reason and scripture will forever sanctify. The citizens of these states have had sense enough to comprehend the full force of these principles, and virtue enough, in the face of uncommon dangers, to act upon so just, so broad, and stable a foundation.[27]

The Lingering Doubt

This passage from Cooper reflects the confidence the clergy members had in their political theory as the founding era drew to a close. The Revolution was successful, the nation's initial Constitutional woes were behind them, and despite the struggle with piety and virtue, the future looked good. Hope radiated from their preaching. Intellectually, they were satisfied with their new political theory. They were not, however, fully at peace with it.

Despite tremendous effort, they had still not resolved the tension between religion and politics. The Congregationalists had erected an enlightened republican government on top of a Puritan base, and they

---

25. Thomas Barnard, *A Sermon Preached at the Request . . .* , 21–22; Joseph Lyman, *A Sermon Preached Before His Excellency James Bowdoin, Esq. . . .* , 55; and, Josiah Bridge, *A Sermon Preached Before His Excellency John Hancock Esq. . . .* , 34–35.
   26. See Howard, *A Sermon Preached Before,* 359–61; and Adams, *A Sermon,* 541–42.
   27. Samuel Cooper, *A Sermon Preached Before His Excellency John Hancock . . .* , 18–19 (emphasis mine); see also Nathaniel Emmons, *The Dignity of Man,* 892–93.

were trying to fuse the two using a cement composed of the covenant and the millennium. They acted as though it would work, but a lingering doubt remained as to whether the cement would hold.

The ministers' primary question focused on whether a liberal notion of religious freedom could be held along with the codification and promotion of a Christian standard of virtue, which included the obligation to support a government-sanctioned religion. Joseph Lathrop, an ardent defender of both Christianity and Congregationalism, tackled the question in his set of miscellaneous essays. First, he argued for the importance of religion to virtue and therefore society.

> To talk of virtue independent of piety, is as absurd in morals, as it is, in nature, to talk of an animal that lives without breath. But how shall a sense of the Deity, his perfections and providence, and a future state, be generally diffused and maintained among a people, so as to become a principle prompting them to virtue, without some publick forms of social worship?[28]

He then affirmed the Congregationalist belief in the liberal understanding of the inviolability of conscience.

> It would be absurd to prescribe certain forms of worship and compel men to conform to *these* and to these *only;* for every man must be at liberty to judge what is truth, and what is the most acceptable way of serving his Maker, and to conduct himself accordingly, provided his conduct no way interferes with the peace and safety of others.[29]

Lathrop then tried to reconcile the two positions by arguing:

> to require an abstinence from the common labours of life one day in seven, and an attendance on the worship of God in some form or other, is no more an invasion on the rights of conscience, than a prohibition of vice or an injunction to maintain the poor and support schools.[30]

According to Lathrop, any rational person could see the correctness of his conclusions. That a rational person could draw a different conclusion was unthinkable. People, however, were beginning to argue for "the unthinkable." Some citizens had already suggested that the requirement of religious worship was a violation of religious conscience and ought to be dropped. This was a serious objection: granting it would mean the loss of Congregationalist hegemony, and separate the state from the covenant. Recognizing the importance of the point, Lathrop attempted to rebut it.

28. Joseph Lathrop, *A Miscellaneous Collection of Original Pieces*, 667.
29. Ibid., 669.
30. Ibid.

> But this . . . would lead us as much to discard the virtues as the vices of
> our fathers; and to reject the whole decalogue as the fourth command-
> ment. . . . Arguments to prove that there ought to be no laws in favour
> of religion, operate alike against all laws in support of learning, virtue
> and good manners, that is, they operate not at all, unless it be in the
> minds of the thoughtless and the undiscerning.[31]

In Lathrop's response we find the contradiction that undergirds eighteenth-century Congregationalist political thought. Lathrop, well trained
in logic and reason, used a logical fallacy to rebut his opponent. He
argued that the implications of complete religious freedom were so
abominable that they could not be rationally asserted. He did not show,
however, what was irrational about it. Just because the consequences
seemed abominable to Lathrop does not resolve the question in his favor.

Lathrop's response, while faulty in logic, was not irrational. Lathrop
clearly saw that if he was wrong, if reason could support disestablishment, it meant that the Congregationalist synthesis was flawed, perhaps
fatally so. If his opponents were correct, if reason and revelation could
be rationally severed, then so could the two essential elements of the
Congregationalist system: the government and the covenant. This was
unacceptable to the ministers. If Lathrop's critics were correct, then a
different constitution would have to be developed, one that would in fact
fuse religion and politics. It is ironic that the Puritan constitution, so long
rejected and reviled, would have met their need.

Lathrop was staring into the face of nineteenth- and twentieth-century
political thought. Rather than confront it, he turned his head, finished
his essay, and assured his readers that reason required religion and
politics to be inextricably linked and praised the efficacy of the Congregationalist constitution. Using Perry Miller's words, Lathrop and his
fellow clergymen stood "on the threshold of an inconceivable age."[32]
The Congregationalists of the next century would witness what was to
Lathrop inconceivable: the rise of secular reason and the destruction of
the Congregationalist polity.

As the founding era closed, however, the Congregationalists were
confident that their position of influence would continue. They were
confident of the quality of their political theory and optimistic about the
future of Massachusetts. Provided that their jeremiads were heard and
the covenant kept, they believed everything was in place to welcome the
millennium.

31. Ibid., 670.
32. Miller, "The Insecurity of Nature," 38.

EPILOGUE

Virtually all the modern world has been read into Calvinism: liberal politics and voluntary associations; capitalism and the social discipline upon which it rests; bureaucracy with its systematic procedures and its putatively diligent and devoted officials; and finally all the routine forms of repression, joylessness, and unrelaxed aspiration. . . . Undoubtedly there is some truth in all these interpretations. . . . It is now necessary to add, however, that this incorporation was a long and complex process, involving selection, corruption, and transformation; it was the result of men working upon their Calvinist heritage.

Michael Walzer

In the epigraph that opens this book, Andrew Eliot summed up the mission of the Massachusetts Congregationalist clergy: to implement heaven's design for politics. Like the Puritans before them, the Massachusetts Congregationalists believed they had discovered the proper structure and design for earthly politics, and as the founding era closed, they looked to the future with millennial hope.

The ministers believed their political theory, at its heart, was Christian. Given their understanding of reason and revelation, and their belief that God left to men the construction of political regimes, it is easy to see why the ministers so freely consulted eighteenth-century political ideas when constructing their political theory. Using Old Testament republican thought as a starting point, they constructed a political theory drawn from a variety of intellectual traditions.

Identifying these traditions with precision is difficult. First, the founding was an era so intellectually pregnant and ideologically diverse that it is difficult to identify the various influences. As Isaac Kramnick points out,

> Problematic . . . is the assumption that there is but one language— one exclusive or even hegemonic paradigm—that characterizes the political discourse of a particular place or moment in time. This was not the case in 1787. In the "great national discussion" of the Constitution, Federalists and Antifederalists, in fact tapped several languages of politics, the terms of which they could easily verbalize. Four such "distinguishable idioms" coexisted in the discourse of American politics

141

in 1787–1788. None dominated the field, and the use of one was compatible with the use of another by the same writer or speaker. There was a profusion and confusion of political tongues among the founders. They lived easily with that clatter; it is we, two hundred and more years later, who chafe at their inconsistency. Reading the framers and the critics of the Constitution, one discerns the languages of republicanism, of Lockean liberalism, or of work-ethic Protestantism, and of state-centered theories of power and sovereignty.[1]

Second, it is even more difficult to isolate and categorize these ideas with the hope of accurately relating them to the larger world of intellectual history. This difficulty is described in Gordon Wood's critique of the liberalism/republican debate:

> The question of which tradition in the late eighteenth century was more dominant—republicanism or liberalism—is badly posed. It assumes a sharp dichotomy between two clearly identifiable traditions that eighteenth-century reality will not support. None of the historical participants, including the Founding Fathers, ever had any sense that he had to choose between republicanism and liberalism, between Machiavelli and Locke. Jefferson could believe simultaneously, and without any sense of inconsistency, in the likelihood of America's becoming corrupt and in the need to protect individual rights from government. These boxlike categories of "classical republicanism" and "liberalism" are the inventions of historians and as such they are distortions of past reality.[2]

Third, to make better judgments concerning intellectual influence, we need to go beyond the clergy's writings and examine the intellectual life of its members. This can be done by studying their college curriculum, letters, personal libraries, and reading material. Unfortunately, we have little knowledge of these. Thomas Siegel and David Robson have given us some sense of the eighteenth-century Harvard curriculum, but the political nature of the curriculum is largely unknown. Moreover, due to the Harvard library fire of 1763, material that could have answered many of these questions is forever lost. Neither can the ministers' personal libraries provide us with much help; we have the papers and records of only a few, and of those, only a few diaries and letters are politically relevant.

Nevertheless, despite these difficulties, we must not conclude that our efforts to understand the intellectual and ideological roots of Massachusetts Congregationalists are in vain. Many of the intellectual

1. Kramnick, *Republicanism*, 261.
2. Gordon S. Wood, "The Virtues and Interests," 34.

traditions overviewed in the introduction to Part I can be found in these sermons.

Ideas reminiscent of the Scottish Enlightenment are evident in the clergy's thinking about human nature and morality. The clergy did not hold a Calvinist or even a Puritan understanding of human depravity, nor did it embrace Locke's epistemology. Instead, the ministers held a view of human nature and moral understanding similar to that of Francis Hutcheson, who asserted, contrary to Locke, "that man's moral sense was innate rather than the product of reason, and that this inborn proclivity ultimately inclined men to sociable and public-regarding behavior."[3] Though the Fall accounted for human moral failure and conflict, the ministers, because of Hutcheson's influence, were more optimistic than their Puritan fathers about the ability of education and reason to transform the human condition. Given the human predisposition toward morality and community, magistrates, ministers, parents, and educators need only acquaint most citizens with the standards of public and private virtue in order to produce behavior supportive of a healthy community. Norman Fiering would not be surprised at this finding. He argued that the "most significant development in the history of ethics between 1675 and 1725" at Harvard was "the rise of sentimentalist ethical theory."[4]

The commitment of the ministers to ideas found in the English Constitution reflects the influence of many strains of republican and Whig thought. Although many Whig ideas also paralleled important Puritan commitments, their influence cannot be overlooked. The ministers were committed to popular sovereignty and republican institutions; they were concerned about virtue, commerce, luxury, corruption, and selfish individualism. Such ideas had great currency in New England, and they must be taken as evidence that the republican tradition played an important role in the ministers' political thinking.

Although liberalism, as Wood pointed out, is a problematic category, the clergy's writings express ideas associated with what would come to be known as liberalism. State of nature theorizing, individual rights, and popular sovereignty all played a prominent role in the ministers' political thinking, as did a liberal conception of the relationship between church and state.

The sermons also reflect the influence of other elements of the Enlightenment. The clergy was well educated and aware of contemporary

3. Donald S. Lutz, "The Intellectual Background to the American Founding," 2337.
4. Fiering, *Moral Philosophy*, 5.

developments in European thought. Although its members did not accept the radical antireligious strain of Voltaire, the Old Lights were party to the Enlightenment project of bringing religion in line with more modern empirical and scientific thinking. The extent of their debt to the Enlightenment goes far beyond politics. The Unitarian/Congregationalist split that occurred in 1800 indicates that the theological and philosophical currents of the Enlightenment were absorbed by many in the Massachusetts clergy.

The influences of Reformed and Puritan thought cannot be overlooked. As Ruth Bloch argues, the interpenetration of religious and ideological themes is so evident in the ministers' thinking that it is wrong to minimize the influence of Calvinist theology.[5] Their emphasis on covenant, the millennium, and virtue demonstrates the continuing significance of the Puritan tradition, albeit in a modified way.

Massachusetts Congregationalist political thought of this period is clearly indebted to a number of intellectual traditions. It is difficult to discern, however, which are most important. The thorniest problem concerns interpreting the ministers' commitment to republicanism and virtue. The sermons use ideas and language that can be interpreted in various ways. Those who see the founding as a Lockean event, those who see it as a liberal event, those who see it as a republican event, and those who see it as a Calvinist event each can claim influence. While all traditions are involved, it is the Reformed tradition that remains dominant.

Massachusetts Congregationalist thought is a fine example of what Michael Walzer calls the corruption and transformation of Calvinism. In the early seventeenth century, Puritan thought was unmistakably Calvinistic. As the eighteenth century drew to a close, however, the corruption and transformation were well on their way to completion. The question is: Where did ministers stand in relation to this process? Were their deepest commitments to their Calvinist roots or to one or more of the Enlightenment traditions? In other words, are they politically enlightened Christians, or have they become Enlightenment thinkers who baptize their thought with Christian imagery?

Although they were no doubt close to a point of transition, it appears that the ministers were Christians first; their political thought can only be understood if their religion is held to be primary. The other traditions

5. Ruth Bloch, "Religion and Ideological Change in the American Revolution," 44–61.

certainly exist in their thinking, but to hold any one of them as primary is to misunderstand their thought.

The Congregationalists were at the same time men of reason and Christians. They believed that piety and virtue mattered to politics and mattered a great deal. They had always been persuaded that there was no ideal polity and had consequently shown flexibility in constitutional form. Although they were ardent supporters of the English Constitution, the American Revolution revealed that their deepest commitments lay elsewhere. Changes had certainly occurred in their political thinking since the *Arbella* landed in Massachusetts Bay, but Calvinist threads pervaded their political thought from 1630 to 1790—limited popular sovereignty, republicanism, piety, virtue, and the political importance of religion.

When the Revolution presented the ministers with a new challenge, a new political theory had to be forged, and the one they created was rooted in these Calvinistic threads. Christianity remained for the Congregationalists, as it had been for the Puritans, of unparalleled importance. What vexed them was trying to create a coherent vision of religion and politics. They found appeal in both the liberal vision of religious freedom and the Puritan desire that religion pervade all of life, including politics.

Although the ministers were enticed by modern ideas and ultimately accepted many modern assumptions, they continued to share with their Puritan fathers a fundamental assumption about the importance of true piety. They agreed with the modern belief that reason provided improving means of governing, that republican government and popular sovereignty were important factors in protecting liberty, and that good laws and education can go a long way toward inculcating virtue. Nevertheless, for them the most important factor in a healthy polity was the Christian religion. The liberal answer enticed them, but it only had appeal so long as Christian piety and virtue remained the foundation of the polity. Consequently, they could never give liberalism their soul.

The covenant remained as important to the Congregationalists as it was to the Puritans, and it continued to form the basis of their political vision. Although the mature Congregationalist constitution may have several similarities with secular republican thought, in the ministers' eyes it was not secular at all. It was a constitution Increase Mather could have supported, or even negotiated, because it was based on a foundation of virtue and piety, with the covenant and the promise of the millennium used to cement them together. The future would show a failure of the cement to bond, but if these ministers had been forced to choose between their present Constitutional theory and the covenant, they would have reexamined their political theory immediately.

Locke, Republicanism, and Virtue?

This interpretation will certainly be questioned by those who hold the primacy of modern and Enlightened thought in the political thinking of these ministers. Defenders of the priority of liberalism and republicanism will undoubtedly question how the primacy of Calvinism, albeit a corrupted one, can be maintained given the acknowledged importance of Locke, Sidney, and other Whig theorists to the ministers.

As Donald Lutz discovered, outside of the Bible, Locke was quoted by the ministers more than any other single theorist, and his *Second Treatise* was quoted more than any other work.[6] Locke's political ideas can be found throughout the sermons, especially his conception of the social contract and its constitutional implications. It cannot be denied that he played an important role in their political thought, especially when one considers that he was a figure with which they were familiar, and in whom they trusted.

The ministers had all become familiar with Locke's *Essay on Human Understanding* at Harvard. More important, they understood Locke as a Christian thinker, not a secular thinker.[7] Modern political theorists often overlook Locke's religious writings, particularly his last major work, *A Paraphrase on the Epistles of St. Paul*. Although there is considerable disagreement concerning the role and importance of religion to Locke, the Congregationalists had no debate. They saw him as one of their own, a Christian intellectual with a Puritan heritage.

Consequently, when the Stamp Act forced ministers to respond instantly, it is not surprising they turned to the ideas of someone they trusted, someone whose intellectual framework they believed themselves to share. Not surprisingly, they found in Locke political ideas that cohered with their worldview, and which they could embrace.

To this degree, we can reaffirm Baldwin's assertion of Locke's importance to the ministers. Such a conclusion would not surprise either John Dunn or Bernard Bailyn, who, in their separate studies, while downplaying Locke's influence in America, have always identified the New

6. Lutz, *A Preface*, 137.

7. John Dunn, *Interpreting Political Responsibility: Essays 1981–1989*, 9–25; John Dunn, *The Political Thought of John Locke: An Historical Account of the Argument of the "Two Treatises of Government";* Winthrop S. Hudson, "John Locke: Heir of Puritan Political Theorists," 108–29.

England clergy as one of the groups that consulted him. Neither does this finding surprise Steven Dworetz, who has made the existence of Locke in sermons of the New England clergy a central portion of his argument for the importance of Locke in American political thought.[8] Nevertheless, contrary to Baldwin and to some degree Dworetz, neither Locke nor liberalism was the primary or sole source of the clergy's political thought. Although Locke was important, his influence was not singular. Several ideas asserted by the clergy cannot be found in Locke, including checks and balances and opposition to standing armies. Undoubtedly, other republican theorists such as Sidney, Trenchard and Gordon, and Cato were also significant resources employed by the clergy.

Although these writers certainly shaped the thought of the clergy, their presence does not require that they and their ideas be accorded a position of intellectual primacy. If Congregationalists had embraced ideas opposed to the foundations of their tradition, an assertion of the primacy of these ideas would have merit. The ministers, however, did not absorb from these thinkers ideas fundamentally at odds with their political heritage. It cannot be denied that these thinkers and the intellectual traditions they represent shaped the thought of the clergy. Their influence shaped but did not remake Congregationalist political thought.

The foundation of eighteenth-century Congregationalist political thought was established in 1691 with the second charter. This is prior to the time in which the theorists and traditions in question would have had much, if any, opportunity to influence the ministers. In fact, if anything is to be made of the parallels between the politics of Congregationalists and their Enlightened counterparts, a more fruitful line of inquiry might be to examine whether the republican theorists have the same Calvinist roots as the clergy. Locke and Sidney certainly do.

Other critics of this interpretation may see the clergy's embrace of republicanism and millennialism as a sign that secular republicanism lay at the heart of the clergy's political vision. Nathan Hatch, for instance, asserts that when considering the political thought of the New England clergy at this time, republicanism, not religion, must be considered dominant:

> Far from being a process that removed the political sector from the domination of religious symbols—a plausible inference from studies that treat this period of religious history primarily in terms of the

8. John Dunn, "The Politics of Locke," 73; Bailyn, *Ideological Origins;* Dworetz, *Unvarnished Doctrine.*

separation of church and state and the rise of religious liberty—this intellectual shift saw the expansion of New England's functional theology to include republican ideas as a primary article of faith. The resulting creed, what might well be called a "republican eschatology," became a surprisingly stable index for interpreting politics in the last third of the century as it translated the most evocative Puritan religious forms according to the grammars of republican values. With the reconstruction of typology depicting Israel as a republic, of the jeremiad portraying early New England as a bulwark against tyranny, and of the millennium envisioning a kingdom of civil and religious liberty, the clergy appropriated the means of traditional religion to accomplish the ends of civic humanism, goals which previously had not been a theological priority.[9]

On the whole, Hatch's study is an extraordinarily fine piece of research that is a valuable resource on Congregationalist history and theology. Nevertheless, as Harry Stout argues, Hatch's conclusion warrants criticism on this point:

> The more one reads these sermons the more one finds unsatisfactory the suggestion that ideas of secular "republicanism," "civil millennialism," or class conscious "popular ideology" were the primary ideological triggers of radical resistance and violence in the Revolution. Such temporal concerns may have motivated other colonists, and they certainly engaged "Americans" after 1776, but they were not the ideological core around which the Revolution in New England revolved. In Revolutionary New England, ministers continued to monopolize public communications, and the terms they most often employed to justify resistance and to instill hope emanated from the Scriptures and from New England's enduring identity as an embattled people of the Word who were commissioned to uphold a sacred and exclusive covenant between themselves and God.[10]

Clearly, republicanism was a "corrupting" influence, but not a new foundation.

Hatch's use of the term "civic humanism," draws attention to a criticism that J. G. A. Pocock and others may have at this juncture: that the clergy's obsession with virtue reflects the influence of pre-Reformation classical republicanism. Although virtue is an important part of republican ideology, the virtue advocated in these sermons is not Machiavellian public virtue, but rather a Reformed vision of Christian virtue.

9. Hatch, *Sacred,* 11–12.
10. Stout, *New England Soul,* 7.

As the introduction pointed out, classical republicanism understands "human beings as political animals who realize themselves only through participation in public life, through active citizenship in a republic."[11] Proponents of this position assert that the "exercise of civic virtue enabled men to realize their human potential at the same time it imposed form on the flotsam and jetsam of human events. Only men secure in their property could be virtuous, and only through the exertions of such men could property be made secure."[12] This position implies that property is a prerequisite to virtue, that public life is the means through which men become virtuous, and that virtue is associated "with self-assertion and self-realization, not with self-abnegation."[13]

The Congregationalist clergy staunchly opposed such an understanding of virtue. Although there is no question that the ministers were, on the whole, Federalists who often supported property interests, their understanding of virtue was rooted in the Christian tradition. They taught that knowledge of virtue is not culturally derived but is obtained by an understanding of the mind of God, consistent with Scripture.

The Congregationalist understanding of virtue, though not completely faithful to Calvin, is rooted in the Calvinist tradition. Calvin, along with the Congregationalists, flatly rejected the classical republican notion that virtue is rooted in a self-interest attached to public activity.

> Calvin's doctrine is more inward than the accounts of philosophers because it demands a holiness absolutely detached from man's natural self-interest, a "life of righteousness to which we are not at all inclined by nature." And since this holiness is alien to our nature we can never achieve "our union with God . . . by virtue of our holiness. . . ." To become a vessel of this divine holiness, the believer must be emptied of all attachment to human goods; as far as possible he must forget himself and all natural virtue.[14]

Like Calvin, Congregationalists did not believe that "true righteousness can be enforced." Nevertheless, they "took it for granted that it was entirely appropriate to urge on magistrates their duty to" encourage "the piety and virtue of the citizenry by means of laws and directives."[15]

In contrast to classical republicanism, virtue was understood not as a creation of the society or the self, but of God. Although virtue certainly

11. Kramnick, *Republicanism*, 164.
12. Appleby, *Liberalism and Republicanism*, 283.
13. Christopher Lasch, *The True and Only Heaven: Progress and Its Critics*, 173.
14. Ralph C. Hancock, *Calvin and the Foundations of Modern Politics*, 93.
15. Harro Höpfl, *The Christian Polity of John Calvin*, 189.

benefits society, its prime purpose and benefit is the satisfaction that it gives God. The Congregationalists' ongoing embrace of the Puritan covenant demonstrates that they continued to hold this understanding of virtue. For Massachusetts and the United States to avoid God's wrath and to flourish, it was essential to have a polity that honored God by promoting a vision of religious liberty and virtuous living rooted in the Reformed tradition. Because Christianity continued to lie at the heart of the ministers' understanding of virtue, the Congregationalist clergy's condemnation of sin and ungodliness in 1679 could have been reproduced verbatim in 1790 with no loss of comprehension or coherence. Indeed, classical republicanism cannot be the source of the Congregationalist understanding of virtue because its understanding of virtue is incompatible with Congregationalist thought. As Christopher Lasch pointed out:

> Recent scholarship, much of it inspired by the hope of reviving a sense of civic obligation and of countering the acquisitive individualism fostered by liberalism, has overlooked the more vigorous concept of virtue that was articulated in certain varieties of radical Protestantism. For a Puritan like John Milton, "virtue" referred not to the disinterested service of the public good but to the courage, vitality, and life-giving force emanating, in the last analysis, from the creator of the universe. Milton associated virtue both with the blessings conferred on mankind by God and with the grateful recognition of life as a gift rather than a challenge to our power to shape it to our own purposes. Jonathan Edwards likewise understood that gratitude implied a recognition of man's dependence on a higher power. For Edwards, ingratitude—the refusal to acknowledge limits on human powers, the wish to achieve godlike knowledge and capacities—became the antithesis of virtue and the essence of original sin.[16]

Massachusetts Congregationalists of this era stand with Milton, Edwards, and the Reformed understanding of virtue.

Barry Alan Shain would not be surprised that Reformed thought would continue to dominate the political thought of the Congregationalists. He found it a significant factor, not just in the politics of this group, but in the founding at large.

> The influence of classical and Renaissance republican authors on the political thought and institutions of late 18th-century Americans, although important, surely was more muted than has been claimed. But if Revolutionary-era Americans were not deeply committed to classical republicanism or incipient individualism, what then provided the foundations on which their political and ethical thought rested?

16. Lasch, *The True,* 15.

The answer is clear. Americans had available to them, aside from these two political visions, alternative ways of viewing political and social life. Most importantly, their political institutions and their understanding of collective human flourishing were shaped by reformed Protestantism.[17]

Although there are clear links between the conclusions of this study and those of Shain, more work needs to be done to discover the extent of Reformed influence in America at this time. Jack Greene has cautioned that one is not to make too much of the politics of New England when discussing America during this era, and his caution is well-advised.

Nevertheless, Greene has also argued for the exceptional character of American thought: Certainly the covenantal theology and politics of the Puritans and Congregationalists qualifies as one of the exceptional features of American colonial and revolutionary politics.[18] Yet even if Congregationalists were exceptional, even if Reformed thought did play a major role in the politics of Massachusetts and perhaps other states during the founding, the persuasive power of Reformed thought was soon to wane. More study is needed to understand the full nature of the influence of Reformed thought at the founding, and the reasons surrounding its subsequent decline.

A full examination of the political decline of Massachusetts Congregationalism in the nineteenth and twentieth centuries has yet to be written, but it would be of great value in examining the declining influence of Reformed political thought in America. Such a study would satisfy not just our historical curiosity, but might also enable us to better understand the nature of some present difficulties that America faces. The history of Congregationalism foreshadows the contemporary debate concerning the relationship between liberalism and virtue. Liberalism has been under heavy attack in recent decades by critics who argue it is incapable of providing the moral foundation a polity needs to survive.[19] Whether or not the assumptions of liberalism render it intellectually and politically incompatible with Christianity and religion in general is a question of profound importance to Christianity, to America, and indeed to Western political thought.

17. Shain, *Myth*, 320–21.
18. Jack P. Greene, *The Intellectual Constitution of America: Exceptionalism and Identity from 1492 to 1800.*
19. See R. Bruce Douglass, Gerald M. Mara, and Henry S. Richardson, eds., *Liberalism and the Good;* Kenneth L. Deutsch and Walter Soffer, eds., *The Crisis of Liberal Democracy: A Straussian Perspective;* William M. Sullivan, *Reconstructing Public Philosophy;* and Christopher Lasch, *The Culture of Narcissism: American Life in an Age of Diminishing Expectations.*

BIBLIOGRAPHY

Primary Sources

1. Collections that Include Sermons

Bailyn, Bernard, and Jane N. Garrett, eds. *Pamphlets of the American Revolution, 1750–1765.* Vol. 1. Cambridge: Harvard University Press, Belknap Press, 1965.

Hyneman, Charles S., and Donald S. Lutz, eds. *American Political Writing during the Founding Era 1760–1805,* 2 vols. Indianapolis: Liberty Press, 1983.

Plumstead, A. W., ed. *The Wall and the Garden.* Minneapolis: University of Minnesota Press, 1968.

Sandoz, Ellis, ed. *Political Sermons of the American Founding Era, 1730–1805.* Indianapolis: Liberty Press, 1991.

Thornton, John Wingate, ed. *The Pulpit of the American Revolution: or, the Political Sermons of the Period of 1776.* Boston: Gould & Lincoln, 1860; New York: Sheldon & Co., 1860; Cincinnati: George S. Blanchard, 1860; New York: Da Capo Press, 1970.

2. Sermons and Pamphlets

Adams, Amos. *A Concise, Historical View of the Perils, Hardships, Difficulties and Discouragements which have Attended the Planting and Progressive Improvements of New England. . . .* Boston: Kneeland & Adams, 1769.

———. *Religious Liberty an Invaluable Blessing. . . .* Boston: Kneeland & Adams, 1768.

Adams, Zabdiel. *The Evil Designs of Men Made Subservient by God to the Public Good.* Boston: Benjamin Edes & Sons, 1783.

———. *The Grounds and Confidence of Success in War. . . .* Boston: Mills & Hicks, 1775.

———. *A Sermon Preached Before His Excellency John Hancock, Esq. . . .* Boston: T. & J. Fleet and J. Gill, n.d.

Appleton, Nathaniel. *The Right Method of Addressing the Divine Majesty in Prayer. . . .* Boston: Edes & Gill, 1770.

———. *A Thanksgiving Sermon on the Total Repeal of the Stamp-Act.* Boston: Edes & Gill, 1766.

Balch, Thomas. *A Sermon Preached to the Ancient and Honorable Artillery Company.* . . . Boston: Edes & Gill, 1763.

Baldwin, Samuel. *A Sermon Preached at Plymouth, December 22, 1775.* . . . Boston: Powars & Willis, 1776.

Barnard, Edward. *A Sermon Preach'd April 12, 1764 on the Public Fast.* . . . Portsmouth, N.H.: Daniel & Robert Fowle, 1764.

————. *A Sermon Preached Before His Excellency Francis Bernard, Esq.* . . . Boston: Richard Draper and Samuel Draper, 1766.

————. *A Sermon Preached Before the Annual Convention of Ministers.* . . . Boston: Kneeland & Davis, 1773.

Barnard, Thomas. *A Sermon Preached at the Request.* . . . Boston: Benjamin Russell, 1789.

————. *A Sermon Preached Before His Excellency Francis Bernard Esq.* . . . Boston: Richard Draper, 1763.

Bascom, Jonathan. *A Sermon Preached at Eastham.* . . . Boston: Edes & Gill, 1775.

Bridge, Ebenezer. *A Sermon Preached Before His Excellency Francis Bernard Esq.* . . . Boston: Green & Russell, 1767.

Bridge, Josiah. *A Sermon Preached Before His Excellency John Hancock Esq.* . . . Boston: Adams & Nourse, 1789.

Browne, John. *A Discourse Delivered on the Day of the Annual Provincial Thanksgiving.* . . . Boston: Thomas & John Fleet, 1771.

Chauncy, Charles. *The Accursed Thing Must be Taken Away From Among a People, If They Would Reasonably Hope to Stand Before their Enemies.* Boston: Thomas & John Fleet, 1778.

————. *A Discourse on "the Good News From a Far Country" Deliver'd July 24th [1766].* . . . Boston: Kneeland & Adams, 1766.

————. *Trust in God, the Duty of a People in a Day of Trouble.* Boston: Daniel Kneeland, 1770.

Clarke, Jonas. *Fate of the Blood-Thirsty Oppressors.* . . . Boston: Powars and Willis, 1776.

————. *The Importance of Military Skill, Measures for Defense and a Martial Spirit, in a Time of Peace.* Boston: Kneeland & Adams, 1768.

————. *A Sermon Preached Before his Excellency John Hancock, Esq.* . . . Boston: J. Gill and Edes & Sons, 1781.

Cleaveland, Ebenezer. *The Abounding Grace of God Toward Notorious Sinners.* . . . Salem, Mass.: S. & E. Hall, 1775.

Conant, Sylvanus. *An Anniversary Sermon Preached at Plymouth, December 23, 1776.* . . . Boston: Thomas & John Fleet, 1777.

Cooke, Samuel. *A Sermon Preached at Cambridge.* . . . Boston: Edes & Gill, 1770.

Cooper, Samuel. *A Place for My People Israel.* Boston: New England Historical and Genealogical Society, 1978.

———. *A Sermon Preached Before His Excellency John Hancock. . . .* Boston:
T. and J. Fleet, 1780.

———. *A Sermon upon Occasion of the Death of our Sovereign George the
Second. . . .* Boston: John Draper, 1761.

Cumings, Henry. *A Sermon Preached at Lexington. . . .* Boston: Benjamin
Edes & Sons, 1781.

———. *A Sermon Preached Before His Honor Thomas Cushing, Esq. . . .* Boston: T. & J. Fleet, 1783.

———. *A Sermon Preached in Billerica, December 11, 1783. . . .* Boston: T. and
J. Fleet, 1784.

———. *A Sermon Preached in Billerica on the 23rd of November, 1775. . . .*
Worcester, Mass.: I. Thomas, n.d.

———. *A Thanksgiving Sermon Preached at Billerica. . . .* Boston: Kneeland
and Adams, 1767.

Cushing, Jacob. *Divine Judgements upon Tyrants: and Compassion to the
Oppressed.* Boston: Powars and Willis, 1778.

Dunbar, Samuel. *The Presence of God with his People, their only Safety and
Happiness.* Boston: S. Kneeland, 1760.

Eliot, Andrew. *A Sermon Preached Before His Excellency Francis Bernard,
Esq. . . .* Boston: Green & Russell, 1765.

Emerson, Joseph. *A Thanksgiving-Sermon Preach'd at Pepperrell. . . .* Boston:
Edes & Gill, 1766.

Emmons, Nathaniel. *The Dignity of Man.* In *Political Sermons of the American
Founding Era,* ed. Ellis Sandoz. Indianapolis: Liberty Press, 1991.

Fish, Elisha. *The Art of War Lawful and Necessary for a Christian People. . . .*
Boston: Thomas & John Fleet, 1774.

———. *A Discourse Delivered at Worcester. . . .* Worcester, Mass.: Isaiah
Thomas, 1771.

———. *Joy and Gladness: A Thanksgiving Discourse. . . .* Providence: Sarah
Goddard, and Co., 1767.

Fiske, Nathan. *The Importance of Righteousness to the Happiness, and the Ten-
dency of Oppression to the Misery of a People. . . .* Boston: John Kneeland,
1774.

———. *An Oration Delivered at Brookfield. . . .* Boston: Thomas & John
Fleet, 1781.

Fitch, Elijah. *A Discourse, the Substance of which was Delivered at Hopkington,
on the Lord's-Day, March 24th, 1776, being the next Sabbath following the
Precipitate Flight of the British Troops from Boston.* Boston: John Boyle,
1776.

Forbes, Eli. *The Dignity and Importance of the Military Character Illustrated.*
Boston: Richard Draper, 1771.

Foster, Daniel. *A Sermon Preached Before his Excellency John Hancock, Esq.* . . .
Boston: Thomas Adams, 1790.

Foxcroft, Thomas. *Grateful Reflexions on the Signal Appearances of Divine
Providence for Great Britain and its Colonies in America, which Diffuse a
General Joy.* Boston: S. Kneeland, 1760.

Frisbie, Levi. *An Oration Delivered at Ipswich.* . . . Boston: E. Russell, 1783.

Gay, Ebenezer. *The Devotions of God's People Adjusted to the Dispensations of
His Providence.* Boston: Richard Draper, 1771.

Gordon, William. *A Discourse Preached December 15th, 1774.* . . . Boston:
Thomas Leverett, 1775.

———. *The Separation of the Jewish Tribes.* . . . Boston: J. Gill, 1777.

———. *A Sermon Preached Before the Honorable House of Representatives.* . . .
Watertown[, Mass.]: Benjamin Edes, 1775.

Haven, Jason. *A Sermon Preached Before His Excellency Sir Francis Bernard.* . . .
Boston: Richard Draper, 1769.

———. *A Sermon Preached To the Ancient and Honorable Artillery Company.* . . .
Boston: Edes and Gill, 1761.

Hemmenway, Moses. *A Sermon Preached Before His Excellency John Hancock,
Esq.* . . . Boston: Benjamin Edes & Sons, 1784.

Hilliard, Timothy. *The Duty of a People Under the Oppression of Man, to
Seek Deliverance from God. The Substance of Two Sermons.* . . . Boston:
Greenleaf's, 1774.

Hitchcock, Gad. *An Election Sermon [1774].* In *American Political Writing,*
ed. Charles S. Hyneman and Donald S. Lutz. Indianapolis: Liberty
Press, 1983.

———. *A Sermon Preached at Plymouth December 22nd, 1774.* . . . Boston:
Edes and Gill, 1775.

Holyoke, Edward. *Integrity and Religion to be Principally Regarded, by such as
Design others to Stations of Publick Trust.* Boston: J. Draper, 1736.

Homer, Jonathan. *The Character and Duties of a Christian Soldier.* . . . Boston: Benjamin Russell, 1790.

Howard, Simeon. *A Sermon Preached Before the Honorable House of Representatives of the State of Massachusetts-Bay.* . . . Boston: John Gill,
1780.

———. *A Sermon Preached to the Ancient and Honorable Artillery Company in
Boston.* . . . In *American Political Writing,* ed. Charles S. Hyneman and
Donald S. Lutz. Indianapolis: Liberty Press, 1983.

Langdon, Samuel. *Government Corrupted by Vice, and Recovered by Righteousness.* In *The Pulpit of the American Revolution,* ed. John Wingate

Thornton. Boston: Gould & Lincoln, 1860; New York: Sheldon & Co., 1860; Cincinnati: George S. Blanchard, 1860; New York: Da Capo Press, 1970.

———. *The Republic of the Israelites as an Example to the American States.* Exeter, N.H.: Lamson & Ramlet, 1788.

Lathrop, John. *A Discourse on the Peace.* . . . Boston: Peter Edes, 1784.

———. *A Discourse Preached December 15th 1774.* . . . Boston: D. Kneeland, 1774.

———. *A Discourse Preached on March the Fifth, 1778.* Boston: Draper and Folsom, 1778.

———. *Innocent Blood Crying to God from the Streets of Boston.* London: n.p., n.d.; repr., Boston: Edes & Gill, 1771.

———. *A Sermon Preached To the Ancient and Honorable Artillery-Company.* . . . Boston: Kneeland and Davis, 1774.

Lathrop, Joseph. *A Miscellaneous Collection of Original Pieces.* In *American Political Writing,* ed. Charles S. Hyneman and Donald S. Lutz. Indianapolis: Liberty Press, 1983.

———. *A Sermon Preached in the First Parish in West-Springfield.* . . . Springfield, Mass.: John Russell, 1787.

Lyman, Joseph. *A Sermon Preached At Hatfield December 15th, 1774.* . . . Boston: Edes & Gill, 1775.

———. *A Sermon Preached Before His Excellency James Bowdoin, Esq.* . . . Boston: Adams and Nourse, n.d.

Maccarty, Thaddeus. *Praise to God, a Duty of Continual Obligation.* Worcester, Mass.: I. Thomas, n.d.

———. *Reformation of Manners, of Absolute Necessity.* . . . Boston: William McAlpine, 1774.

Mather, Samuel. *Of the Pastoral Care: A Sermon.* . . . Boston: Thomas & John Fleet, 1762.

Mayhew, Jonathan. *A Discourse Concerning the Unlimited Submission and Non-Resistance to the Higher Powers.* . . . Boston: D. Fowle, 1750; repr., Boston: Hall & Goss, 1818.

———. *Observations on the Charter and Conduct of the Society for the Propagation of the Gospel in Foreign Parts.* Boston: Richard & Samuel Draper, Edes & Gill, and Thomas & John Fleet, 1763.

———. *A Sermon Preach'd in the Audience of His Excellency William Shirley, Esq.* . . . Boston: Samuel Kneeland, 1754.

———. *The Snare Broken, a Thanksgiving Discourse.* . . . Boston: R & S Draper, Edes & Gill, and T & J Fleet, 1766.

Noble, Oliver. *Some Strictures Upon the Sacred Story Recorded in the Book of Esther.* . . . Newburyport, Mass.: E. Lunt & H. W. Tinges, 1775.

Osgood, David. *Reflections on the Goodness of God in Supporting the People of the United States through the Late War, and Giving them so Advantageous and Honorable a Peace.* . . . Boston: T. & J. Fleet, 1784.

————. *A Sermon Preached at the Request of the Ancient and Honorable Artillery Company.* . . . Boston: Benjamin Russell, 1788.

Parsons, David. *A Sermon Preached Before His Excellency John Hancock, Esq.* . . . Boston: Adams & Nourse, n.d.

Parsons, Moses. *A Sermon Preached at Cambridge.* . . . Boston: Edes & Gill, 1772.

Patten, William. *A Discourse Delivered at Hallifax.* . . . Boston: D. Knccland, 1766.

Payson, Phillips. *A Memorial of Lexington Battle.* . . . Boston: Benjamin Edes & Sons, 1782.

————. *A Sermon Preached Before the Honorable Council.* . . . Boston: John Gill, 1778.

Porter, Eliphalet. *A Sermon Delivered to the First Religious Society in Roxbury.* . . . Boston: Adams & Nourse, 1784.

[Prescott, Benjamin]. *A Free and Calm Consideration.* . . . Salem, Mass.: S. & E. Hall, 1774.

Robbins, Nathanael. *Jerusalem's Peace Wished.* Boston: J. Boyles, 1772.

Sampson, Ezra. *A Sermon Preached at Roxbury-Camp, Before Col. Cotton's Regiment.* . . . Watertown: Benjamin Edes, 1775.

A Sermon Prepared Soon After the Boston Massacre, March 5, 1770. Sermons Collection, 1 envelope, Congregational Library (Boston).

Shute, Daniel. *An Election Sermon [1768].* In *American Political Writing,* ed. Charles S. Hyneman and Donald S. Lutz. Indianapolis: Liberty Press, 1983.

————. *A Sermon Preached to the Ancient and Honorable Artillery Company.* . . . Boston: Edes & Gill, 1767.

Spring, Samuel. *A Sermon Delivered at the North Congregational Church in Newbury-port.* . . . . Newbury-port, Mass.: John Mycall, 1778.

Stevens, Benjamin. *A Sermon Preached at Boston, Before the Great and General Court or Assembly.* . . . Boston: John Draper, 1761.

Story, Isaac. *The Love of our Country Recommended and Enforced.* Boston: John Boyle, 1775.

Symmes, William. *A Sermon Preached Before His Honor Thomas Cushing, Esq.* . . . Boston: Adams & Nourse, n.d.

Tappan, David. *A Discourse Delivered at the Third Parish in Newbury.* . . . Salem, Mass.: Samuel Hall, 1783.

Thatcher, Peter. *An Oration Delivered at Watertown, March 5, 1776.* . . . Watertown[, Mass.]: n.p., 1776.

Tucker, John. *An Election Sermon [1771].* In *American Political Writing,* ed. Charles S. Hyneman and Donald S. Lutz. Indianapolis: Liberty Press, 1983.

———. *Ministers Considered as Fellow-workers, who should be Comforters to each other, in the Kingdom of God.* Boston: Thomas & John Fleet, 1768.

Turner, Charles. *Due Glory to be Given to God.* Boston: T. & J. Fleet, 1783.

———. *A Sermon Preached at Plymouth, December 22d, 1773.* . . . Boston: Greenleaf's, 1774.

———. *A Sermon Preached Before His Excellency Thomas Hutchins, Esq.* . . . Boston: Richard Draper, 1773.

Webster, Samuel. *The Misery and Duty of an Oppress'd and Enslav'd People.* . . . Boston: Edes & Gill, 1774.

———. *A Sermon Preached Before the Council.* . . . Boston: Edes & Gill, 1777.

West, Samuel (Needham). *A Sermon, Preached Before His Excellency James Bowdoin, Esq.* . . . Boston: Adams & Nourse, n.d.

———. *A Sermon Preached at the Ordination of the Rev'd Jonathan Newell.* . . . Boston: Edes & Gill, 1775.

West, Samuel. *An Anniversary Sermon Preached at Plymouth, December 22d, 1777.* . . . Boston: Draper & Folsom, 1778.

———. *On the Right to Rebel Against Governors.* In *American Political Writing,* ed. Charles S. Hyneman and Donald S. Lutz. Indianapolis: Liberty Press, 1983.

Whitney, Peter. *American Independence Vindicated.* Boston: E. Draper, 1777.

———. *The Transgressions of a Land Punished by a Multitude of Rulers.* Boston: John Boyle, 1774.

Willard, Joseph. *A Thanksgiving Sermon Delivered at Boston December 11, 1783.* . . . . Boston: T. & J. Fleet, 1784.

Williams, Abraham. *An Election Sermon [1762].* In *American Political Writing,* ed. Charles S. Hyneman and Donald S. Lutz. Indianapolis: Liberty Press, 1983.

Williams, Samuel. *A Discourse on the Love of our Country.* . . . Salem, Mass.: Samuel and Ebenezer Hall, 1775.

———. *The Influence of Christianity on Civil Society.* . . . Boston: John Boyle, 1780.

Wise, John. *The Churches' Quarrel Espoused.* . . . Boston: Congregational Board of Publication, 1860.

———. *Vindication of the Government of New England Churches.* . . . Boston: J. Allen, 1717.

Woodward, Samuel. *The Help of the Lord, in Signal Deliverances and Special Salvations, to be Acknowledged and Remembered.* Boston: John Gill, 1779.

3. Other Primary Sources

Addison, Joseph. *The Freeholder.* Ed. James Lenehy. Oxford: Oxford University Press, Clarendon Press, 1979.

Calvin, John. *The Epistles of Paul the Apostle to the Romans and to the Thessalonians.* Edinburgh: Saint Andrew Press, 1961.

Cole, Franklin P., ed. *They Preached Liberty: An Anthology of Timely Quotations from New England Ministers. . . .* New York: Fleming H. Revell Co., 1941.

Cooper, Samuel. "Samuel Cooper to Thomas Pownall," March 26, 1770. Reprinted in *American Historical Review* 8 (1902–1903): 316–18.

———. "Samuel Cooper to Thomas Pownall," November 14, 1771. Reprinted in *American Historical Review* 8 (1902–1903): 325–26.

Evans, Charles, comp. *American Bibliography: A Chronological Dictionary of All Books, Pamphlets and Periodical Publications Printed in the United States of America [1639–1800].* 14 vols. Chicago: C. Evans, 1903–1959.

The Geneva Bible: The Annotated New Testament, 1602 ed. Cleveland: Pilgrim Press, 1989.

Gordon, William. *The History of the Rise, Progress, and Establishment of the Independence of the United States of America. . . .* London: n.p., 1788.

Greene, Jack P., ed. *Colonies to Nation, 1763–1789: A Documentary History of the American Revolution.* New York: W. W. Norton, 1975.

Hamilton, Alexander, John Jay, and James Madison. *The Federalist Papers.* New York: Mentor, 1961.

Handlin, Oscar, and Mary Handlin, eds. *The Popular Sources of Political Authority: Documents on the Massachusetts Constitution of 1780.* Cambridge: Harvard University Press, Belknap Press, 1966.

Jefferson, Thomas. *Writings.* Comp. Merrill D. Peterson. New York: Literary Classics of the United States, 1984.

Locke, John. *Essays on the Law of Nature.* Ed. W. von Leyden. New York: Oxford University Press, Clarendon Press, 1954.

———. *A Letter Concerning Toleration.* Ed. James H. Tully. Indianapolis: Hackett Publishing Co., 1983.

———. *A Paraphrase and Notes on the Epistles of St Paul to the Galatians, 1 and 2 Corinthians, Romans, Ephesians.* 2 vols. Ed. Arthur Wainwright. Oxford: Clarendon Press, 1987.

———. *The Reasonableness of Christianity As Delivered in the Scriptures,* ed. George W. Ewing. Washington, D.C.: Regnery Gateway, 1965.

———. *Second Treatise of Government.* Ed. C. B. MacPherson. Indianapolis: Hackett, 1980.

Madison, James. *Notes of Debates in the Federal Convention of 1787*. Athens: Ohio University Press, 1985.

Miller, Perry, and Thomas H. Johnson. eds. *The Puritans*. New York: American Book Co., 1938.

Morgan, Edmund, ed. *Puritan Political Ideas, 1558–1794*. Indianapolis: Bobbs-Merrill Co., 1965.

Paine, Thomas. *Common Sense*. Ed. Isaac Kramnick. London: Penguin Books, 1986.

Pope, Alexander. *The Poems of Alexander Pope*. Ed. John Butt. New Haven: Yale University Press, 1974.

Pufendorf, Samuel. *The Classics of International Law*, vol. 2, *De Jure Naturae et Gentium Libri Octo*. Ed. James Brown Scott, trans. C. H. Oldfather and W. A. Oldfather. Oxford: Clarendon Press; London: Humphrey Milford, 1934.

Sidney, Algernon. *Discourses Concerning Government*. Ed. Thomas G. West. Indianapolis: Liberty Classics, 1990.

Smith, Adam. *The Theory of Moral Sentiments*. Ed. D. D. Raphael and A. L. Macfie. Indianapolis: Liberty Classics, 1982.

[Trenchard, John, and Thomas Gordon]. *Cato's Letters; or Essays on Liberty, Civil and Religious*. 3d ed., 4 vols. (1755; reprint, New York: Russell & Russell, 1969).

Walker, Williston. *The Creeds and Platforms of Congregationalism*. New York: Pilgrim Press, 1991.

Williams, E. Neville. *The Eighteenth-Century Constitution, 1688–1815: Documents and Commentary*. Cambridge: Cambridge University Press, 1960.

Wooten, David, ed. *Divine Right and Democracy: An Anthology of Political Writing in Stuart England*. London: Penguin Books, 1986.

Secondary Sources

Aaron, Richard I. *John Locke*. New York: Oxford University Press, Clarendon Press, 1971.

Adair, Douglass, and John A. Schutz, eds. *Peter Oliver's Origin and Progress of the American Rebellion: A Tory View*. Stanford: Stanford University Press, 1961.

Adams, Brooks. *The Emancipation of Massachusetts*. Boston: Houghton Mifflin, 1962.

Ahlstrom, Sydney E. *A Religious History of the American People*. New Haven: Yale University Press, 1972.

Akers, Charles W. *Called unto Liberty: A Life of Jonathan Mayhew, 1720–1766*. Cambridge: Harvard University Press, 1964.

——. *The Divine Politician: Samuel Cooper and the American Revolution in Boston.* Boston: Northeastern University Press, 1982.

Anderson, Marvin W. "The Geneva (Tomson/Junius) New Testament among Other English Bibles of the Period." In *The Geneva Bible.* Cleveland: Pilgrim Press, 1989.

Appleby, Joyce. *Liberalism and Republicanism in the Historical Imagination.* Cambridge: Harvard University Press, 1992.

Aronoff, Myron J., ed. *Religion and Politics.* Political Anthropology Series. New Brunswick, N.J.: Transaction Books, 1984.

Ashcraft, Richard. *Locke's Two Treatises of Government.* London: Unwin Hyman, 1989.

Bailyn, Bernard. *The Ideological Origins of the American Revolution.* Cambridge: Harvard University Press, Belknap Press, 1967.

——. *The Ordeal of Thomas Hutchinson.* Cambridge: Harvard University Press, Belknap Press, 1974.

——. *The Origins of American Politics.* New York: Random House, Vintage Books, 1968.

——. "Religion and Revolution: Three Biographical Studies." *Perspectives in American History* 4 (1970): 83–169.

Baldwin, Alice M. *The New England Clergy and the American Revolution.* Durham: Duke University Press, 1928.

Ball, Terence, and J. G. A. Pocock, eds. *Conceptual Change and the Constitution.* Lawrence: University Press of Kansas, 1988.

Beard, Charles A. *An Economic Interpretation of the Constitution of the United States.* New York: Macmillan Co., 1949.

✓ Becker, Carl. *The Declaration of Independence: A Study in the History of Political Ideas.* New York: Alfred A. Knopf, 1945.

——. *The Heavenly City of the Eighteenth-Century Philosophers.* New Haven: Yale University Press, 1960.

Bercovitch, Sacvan. *The American Jeremiad.* Madison: University of Wisconsin Press, 1978.

Berman, Harold J. *Law and Revolution: The Formation of the Western Legal Tradition.* Cambridge: Harvard University Press, 1983.

Bliss, Robert M. *Revolution and Empire: English Politics and the American Colonies in the Seventeenth Century.* Manchester: Manchester University Press, 1990.

Bloch, Ruth H. "Religion and Ideological Change in the American Revolution." In *Religion and American Politics: From the Colonial Period to the 1980s,* ed. Mark A. Noll. Oxford: Oxford University Press, 1990.

————. *Visionary Republic: Millennial Themes in American Thought, 1756–1800*. Cambridge: Cambridge University Press, 1985.

Bloom, Allan, ed. *Confronting the Constitution: The Challenge to Locke, Montesquieu, Jefferson, and* . . . . Washington, D.C.: AEI Press, 1990.

Bock, Gisela, Quentin Skinner, and Maurizio Viroli, eds. *Machiavelli and Republicanism*. Cambridge: Cambridge University Press, 1990.

Bonomi, Patricia U. *Under the Cope of Heaven: Religion, Society and Politics in Colonial America*. New York: Oxford University Press, 1986.

Bozeman, Theodore Dwight. *To Live Ancient Lives: The Primitivist Dimension in Puritanism*. Williamsburg: Institute of Early American History and Culture; Chapel Hill: University of North Carolina Press, 1988.

Bradford, M. E. *"Against the Barbarians" and Other Reflections on Familiar Themes*. Columbia: University of Missouri Press, 1992.

Breen, T. H. *The Character of the Good Ruler: A Study of Puritan Political Ideas in New England, 1630–1730*. New York: W. W. Norton; New Haven: Yale University Press, 1970.

Bremer, Francis J., ed. *Puritanism: Transatlantic Perspectives on a Seventeenth-Century Anglo-American Faith*. Boston: Northeastern University Press, 1993.

Bridenbaugh, Carl. *Mitre and Sceptre: Transatlantic Faiths, Ideas, Personalities, and Politics 1689–1775*. New York: Oxford University Press, 1962.

Brown, Richard D. "Spreading the Word: Rural Clergymen and the Communication Network of 18th-Century New England." *Massachusetts Historical Society Proceedings* 94 (1984): 1–14.

Brown, Robert E. *Charles Beard and the Constitution: A Critical Analysis of "An Economic Interpretation of the Constitution."* Princeton: Princeton University Press, 1956.

Cliffe, J. T. *The Puritan Gentry: The Great Puritan Families of Early Stuart England*. London: Routledge and Kegan Paul, 1984.

Colbourn, H. Trevor. *The Lamp of Experience: Whig History and the Intellectual Origins of the American Revolution*. Williamsburg: Institute of Early American History and Culture; Chapel Hill: University of North Carolina Press, 1965.

Counts, Martha Louise. "The Political Views of the Eighteenth-Century New England Clergy as Expressed in Their Election Sermons." Ph.D. diss., Columbia University, 1956.

Cousins, Norman, ed. *The Republic of Reason: The Personal Philosophies of the Founding Fathers*. San Francisco: Harper and Row, 1988.

Cranston, Maurice. *John Locke: A Biography*. London: Longmans, 1959.

Crimmins, James E., ed. *Religion, Secularization and Political Thought: Thomas Hobbes to J. S. Mill.* London: Routledge, 1989.

Damico, Alfonso J., ed. *Liberals on Liberalism.* Totowa, N.J.: Rowman and Littlefield, 1986.

Deane, Herbert. *The Political and Social Ideas of St. Augustine.* New York: Columbia University Press, 1963.

Deutsch, Kenneth L., and Walter Soffer, eds. *The Crisis of Liberal Democracy: A Straussian Perspective.* Albany: State University of New York, 1987.

Dexter, Henry Martyn. *Congregationalism: What it is; Whence it is; How it Works. . . .* Boston: Noyes, Holmes, & Co., 1871.

———. *The Congregationalism of the Last Three Hundred Years, as Seen in Its Literature. . . .* New York: Harper & Brothers, 1880.

Diggins, John Patrick. *The Lost Soul of American Politics: Virtue, Self-Interest, and the Foundations of Liberalism.* Chicago: University of Chicago Press, 1984.

Douglass, R. Bruce, Gerald M. Mara, and Henry S. Richardson, eds. *Liberalism and the Good.* New York: Routledge, 1990.

Dunn, John. *Interpreting Political Responsibility: Essays, 1981–1989.* Cambridge: Polity Press, 1990.

———. Interview by author, May 27, 1992. Cambridge, England, notes by author.

———. *Locke.* New York: Oxford University Press, 1984.

———. *The Political Thought of John Locke: An Historical Account of the Argument of the "Two Treatises of Government."* Cambridge: Cambridge University Press, 1969.

———. "The Politics of Locke in England and America in the Eighteenth Century." In *John Locke: Problems and Perspectives: A Collection of New Essays,* ed. John W. Youlton. Cambridge: Cambridge University Press, 1969.

Dworetz, Steven M. Review of *Republicanism and Bourgeois Radicalism: Political Ideology in Late Eighteenth-Century England and America,* by Isaac Kramnick. In *The Journal of Politics* 52 (November 1991): 1199–202.

———. *The Unvarnished Doctrine: Locke, Liberalism, and the American Revolution.* Durham: Duke University Press, 1990.

Eggleston, Edward. *The Transit of Civilization from England to America in the Seventeenth Century.* New York: D. Appleton and Co., 1901.

Eidsmoe, John. *Christianity and the Constitution: The Faith of Our Founding Fathers.* Grand Rapids, Mich.: Baker Book House, 1987.

Eisenach, Eldon J. *Two Worlds of Liberalism: Religion and Politics in Hobbes, Locke, and Mill.* Chicago: University of Chicago Press, 1981.

Elliott, Emory. *Power and the Pulpit in Puritan New England.* Princeton: Princeton University Press, 1975.

Emerson, Everett. "Calvin and Covenant Theology." *Church History* 25 (June 1956) 136–44.

Fiering, Norman. *Jonathan Edwards's Moral Thought and Its British Context.* Chapel Hill: University of North Carolina Press, 1981.

———. *Moral Philosophy at Seventeenth-Century Harvard: A Discipline in Transition.* Chapel Hill: University of North Carolina Press, 1981.

Figgis, John Neville. *The Divine Right of Kings.* Gloucester, Mass.: Peter Smith, 1970.

Fink, Z. S. *The Classical Republicans.* Evanston, Ill.: Northwestern University Press, 1949.

Flower, Elizabeth, and Murray G. Murphey. *A History of Philosophy in America.* 2 vols. New York: Capricorn Books and G. P. Putnam's Sons, 1977.

Formisano, Ronald P. *The Transformation of Political Culture: Massachusetts Parties, 1790s-1840s.* New York: Oxford University Press, 1983.

Forster, Robert, and Jack P. Greene, eds. *Preconditions of Revolution in Early Modern Europe.* Baltimore: Johns Hopkins University Press, 1970.

Foster, Frank Hugh. *A Genetic History of the New England Theology.* Chicago: University of Chicago Press, 1907.

Foster, Stephen, *The Long Argument: English Puritanism and the Shaping of New England Culture, 1570–1700.* Williamsburg: Institute of Early American History and Culture; Chapel Hill: University of North Carolina Press, 1991.

———. "Not What But How—Thomas Minor and the Ligatures of Puritanism." In *Puritanism: Transatlantic Perspectives on a Seventeenth-Century Anglo-American Faith,* ed. Francis J. Bremer, 30–54. Boston: Northeastern University Press, 1993.

Fraser, Alexander Campbell. *Locke.* Philadelphia: J. B. Lippincott Co., n.d.; Edinburgh: Wm. Blackwood & Sons, n.d.

Freeden, Michael. *The New Liberalism: An Ideology of Social Reform.* Oxford: Clarendon Press, 1978.

Galston, William A. *Liberal Purposes: Goods, Virtues, and Diversity in the Liberal State.* Cambridge: Cambridge University Press, 1992.

Gambrell, Mary Latimer. *Ministerial Training in Eighteenth-Century New England.* New York: Columbia University Press, 1937.

Garrett, John. *Roger Williams: Witness Beyond Christendom, 1603–1683.* London: Macmillan Co., 1970.

Gaustad, Edwin S. *Faith of Our Fathers: Religion and the New Nation*. San Francisco: Harper and Row, 1987.

Gerber, Larry G. *The Limits of Liberalism: Josephus Daniels, Henry Stimson, Bernard Baruch, Donald Richberg, Felix Frankfurter and the Development of the Modern Political Economy*. New York and London: New York University Press, 1983.

Goldwin, Robert A., and William A. Schambra, eds. *How Democratic Is the Constitution?* Washington, D.C.: AEI Press, 1980.

Goodhue, Albert, Jr. "The Reading of Harvard Students, 1770–1781, as Shown by the Records of the Speaking Club." *Essex Institute Historical Collections* 73 (April 1937): 107–29.

Gray, John. *Liberalism*. Minneapolis: University of Minnesota Press, 1986.

Greene, Jack P. *The Intellectual Construction of America: Exceptionalism and Identity from 1492 to 1800*. Chapel Hill: University of North Carolina Press, 1993.

———. *Peripheries and Center: Constitutional Development in the Extended Polities of the British Empire and the United States, 1607–1788*. Athens, Ga.: University of Georgia Press, 1986.

———. *Pursuits of Happiness: The Social Development of Early Modern British Colonies and the Formation of American Culture*. Chapel Hill: University of North Carolina Press, 1988.

———, ed. *The American Revolution: Its Character and Limits*. New York: New York University Press, 1987.

Greene, Jack P., and William G. McLoughlin. *Preachers and Politicians: Two Essays on the Origins of the American Revolution*. Worcester, Mass.: American Antiquarian Society, 1977.

Greene, Jack P., and J. R. Pole, eds. *Colonial British America: Essays in the New History of the Early Modern Era*. Baltimore: Johns Hopkins University Press, 1984.

Greven, Philip. *The Protestant Temperament: Patterns of Child-Rearing, Religious Experience, and the Self in Early America*. New York: Alfred A. Knopf, 1977.

Griffin, Edward G. *Old Brick: Charles Chauncy of Boston, 1705–1787*. Minneapolis: University of Minnesota Press, 1980.

Gross, Robert A. *The Minutemen and Their World*. New York: Hill and Wang, 1976.

Hall, David D., *The Faithful Shepherd: A History of the New England Ministry in the Seventeenth Century*. Williamsburg: Institute of Early American History and Culture; Chapel Hill: University of North Carolina Press, 1972.

Hall, Michael G., Lawrence H. Leder, and Michael G. Kammen, eds. *The Glorious Revolution in America: Documents of the Colonial Crisis of 1689.* Chapel Hill, N.C.: University of North Carolina Press, 1964.

Hall, Richard A. S. *The Neglected Northampton Texts of Jonathan Edwards: Edwards on Society and Politics.* Lewiston, N.Y.: Edwin Mellen Press, 1990.

Haller, William. *The Rise of Puritanism.* . . . New York: Harper and Brothers, 1938.

Hambrick-Stowe, Charles E. *The Practice of Piety: Puritan Devotional Disciplines in Seventeenth-Century New England.* Williamsburg: Institute of Early American History and Culture; Chapel Hill: University of North Carolina Press, 1982.

Hamowy, Ronald. "Jefferson and the Scottish Enlightenment: A Critique of Garry Wills's *Inventing America: Jefferson's Declaration of Independence.*" *William and Mary Quarterly* 36 (October 1979): 503–23.

————. Review of *The Unvarnished Doctrine: Locke, Liberalism, and the American Revolution,* by Steven M. Dworetz. In *American Historical Review* 96 (October 1991): 1288–89.

Hancock, Ralph C. *Calvin and the Foundations of Modern Politics.* Ithaca: Cornell University Press, 1989.

Hart, Benjamin. *Faith and Freedom: The Christian Roots of American Liberty.* Dallas: Lewis and Stanley, 1988.

Hartz, Louis. *The Liberal Tradition in America: An Interpretation of American Political Thought since the Revolution.* New York: Harcourt, Brace and World, 1955.

Hatch, Nathan O. *The Sacred Cause of Liberty: Republican Thought and the Millennium in Revolutionary New England.* New Haven: Yale University Press, 1977.

Hatch, Nathan O., and Mark A. Noll, eds. *The Bible in America: Essays in Cultural History.* New York: Oxford University Press, 1982.

Hatch, Nathan O., and Harry S. Stout, eds. *Jonathan Edwards and the American Experience.* New York: Oxford University Press, 1988.

Heimert, Alan. *Religion and the American Mind: From the Great Awakening to the Revolution.* Cambridge: Harvard University Press, 1966.

Herbert, Jerry S., ed. *America, Christian or Secular? Readings in American Christian History and Civil Religion.* Portland, Ore.: Multnomah Press, 1984.

Hill, Christopher. *The English Bible and the Seventeenth-Century Revolution.* London: Penguin Press, 1993.

Hobhouse, L. T. *Liberalism.* New York: Oxford University Press, 1964.

Hont, Istvan, and Michael Ignatieff, eds. *Wealth and Virtue: The Shaping of Political Economy in the Scottish Enlightenment.* Cambridge: Cambridge University Press, 1983.

Höpfl, Harro. *The Christian Polity of John Calvin.* Cambridge: Cambridge University Press, 1985.

Houston, Alan Craig. *Algernon Sidney and the Republican Heritage in England and America.* Princeton: Princeton University Press, 1991.

Howe, Daniel Walker. *The Unitarian Conscience: Harvard Moral Philosophy, 1805–1861.* Middletown, Conn.: Wesleyan University Press, 1988.

Howell, Wilbur Samuel. "The Declaration of Independence and Eighteenth-Century Logic." *William and Mary Quarterly* 18 (October 1961): 463–84.

Hunt, George L., ed. *Calvinism and the Political Order.* Philadelphia: Westminster Press, 1964.

Hudson, Winthrop S. *American Protestantism.* Chicago: University of Chicago Press, 1961.

———. "John Locke: Heir of Puritan Political Theorists." In *Calvinism and the Political Order,* ed. George L. Hunt. Philadelphia: Westminster Press, 1964.

———. *Religion in America.* New York: Charles Scribner's Sons, 1981.

Huyler, Jerome. *Locke in America: The Moral Philosophy of the Founding Era.* Lawrence: University Press of Kansas, 1995.

Jedrey, Christopher M. *The World of John Cleaveland: Family and Community in Eighteenth-Century New England.* New York: W. W. Norton, 1979.

Jenkins, John J. *Understanding Locke: An Introduction to Philosophy through John Locke's Essay.* Edinburgh: Edinburgh University Press, 1983.

Jones, J. R. *The First Whigs: The Politics of the Exclusion Crisis 1678–1683.* Westport, Conn.: Greenwood Press, 1985.

Kaladin, Arthur. "The Mind of John Leverett." Ph.D. diss., Harvard University, 1965.

Kammen, Michael. *People of Paradox: An Inquiry Concerning the Origins of American Civilization.* New York: Alfred A. Knopf, 1973.

Kendall, Willmoore, and George W. Carey. *The Basic Symbols of the American Political Tradition.* Baton Rouge: Louisiana State University Press, 1970.

Kerr, Harry Price. "The Character of Political Sermons Preached at the Time of the American Revolution." Ph.D. diss., Cornell University, 1962.

King, H. Roger. *Cape Cod and Plymouth Colony in the Seventeenth Century.* Lanham, Md.: University Press of America, 1994.

Kirk, Russell. *The Conservative Mind from Burke to Eliot.* 7th rev. ed. Chicago: Regnery Books, 1986.

―――. *The Roots of American Order.* Malibu, Calif.: Pepperdine University Press, 1978.

Kline, Meredith G. *The Structure of Biblical Authority.* Grand Rapids, Mich.: William B. Eerdmans, 1972.

Knight, Janice. *Orthodoxies in Massachusetts: Rereading American Puritanism.* Cambridge: Harvard University Press, 1994.

Koch, Adrienne, ed. *The American Enlightenment: The Shaping of the American Experiment and a Free Society.* New York: George Braziller, 1965.

Kramnick, Isaac. *Republicanism and Bourgeois Radicalism: Political Ideology in Late Eighteenth-Century England and America.* Ithaca: Cornell University Press, 1990.

Kraus, Joe Walker. "Book Collections of Five Colonial College Libraries: A Subject Analysis." Ph.D. diss., University of Illinois, 1960.

Kuklick, Bruce. *Churchmen and Philosophers from Jonathan Edwards to John Dewey.* New Haven: Yale University Press, 1985.

―――. *The Rise of American Philosophy: Cambridge, Massachusetts 1860–1930.* New Haven: Yale University Press, 1977.

Lake, Peter. "Defining Puritanism—Again?" In *Puritanism: Transatlantic Perspectives on a Seventeenth-Century Anglo-American Faith,* ed. Francis J. Bremer, 3–29. Boston: Northeastern University Press, 1993.

Lasch, Christopher. *The Culture of Narcissism: American Life in an Age of Diminishing Expectations.* New York: W. W. Norton, 1979.

―――. *The True and Only Heaven: Progress and Its Critics.* New York: W. W. Norton, 1991.

Laslett, Peter. *John Locke's Two Treatises on Government.* Cambridge: Cambridge University Press, 1960.

Lerner, Ralph. "Believers and the Founders' Constitution." (photocopy), 1988.

Levy, Leonard W. *Essays on the Making of the Constitution.* New York: Oxford University Press, 1987.

Lienesch, Michael. *New Order of the Ages: Time, the Constitution, and the Making of Modern American Political Thought.* Princeton: Princeton University Press, 1988.

Lipset, Seymour Martin. *The First New Nation: The United States in Historical and Comparative Perspective.* New York: Basic Books, 1963.

Loring, James Spear. *The Hundred Boston Orators. . . .* Boston: J. P. Jewett & Co., 1853.

Love, W[illiam] DeLoss. *The Fast and Thanksgiving Days of New England.* Boston: Houghton, Mifflin & Co., 1895.

Lovejoy, David S. *The Glorious Revolution in America.* New York: Harper and Row, 1972.

Lundberg, David, and Henry F. May. "The Enlightened Reader in America." *American Quarterly* 28 (Summer 1976): 262–94.

Lutz, Donald S. "The Intellectual Background to the American Founding." *Texas Tech Law Review* 21 (1990): 2327–48.

———. *The Origins of American Constitutionalism.* Baton Rouge: Louisiana State University Press, 1988.

———. *A Preface to American Political Theory.* Lawrence: University Press of Kansas, 1992.

Lutz, Donald S., and Jack D. Warren. *A Covenanted People: The Religious Traditions and the Origins of American Constitutionalism.* Providence, R.I.: The John Carter Brown Library, 1987.

Lynd, Staughton. *Class Conflict, Slavery, and the United States Constitution: Ten Essays.* Indianapolis: Howard W. Sams and Co., Bobbs-Merrill Co., 1967.

———. *Intellectual Origins of American Radicalism.* Cambridge: Harvard University Press, 1982.

Maclear, J. F. "Isaac Watts and the Idea of Public Religion." *Journal of the History of Ideas* 53 (January–March 1992): 25–45.

Maier, Pauline. *From Resistance to Revolution: Colonial Radicals and the Development of American Opposition to Britain, 1765–1776.* New York: Alfred A. Knopf, 1973.

———. "A Pearl in a Gnarled Shell: Gordon S. Wood's *The Creation of the American Republic* Reconsidered." *William and Mary Quarterly* 44 (July 1987): 583–90.

Maitland, F. W. *The Constitutional History of England: A Course of Lectures Delivered.* Cambridge: Cambridge University Press, 1920.

Mansfield, Harvey C., Jr. *The Spirit of Liberalism.* Cambridge: Harvard University Press, 1978.

Marty, Martin E. *Pilgrims in Their Own Land: 500 Years of Religion in America.* New York: Penguin Books, 1984.

———. "Reformed America and America Reformed." *Reformed Journal* (March 1989) 8–11.

May, Henry F. *The Enlightenment in America.* Oxford: Oxford University Press, 1978.

McDonald, Forrest. *E Pluribus Unum: The Formation of the American Republic, 1776–1790.* 2d ed. Indianapolis: Liberty Press, 1979.

———. *Novus Ordo Seclorum: The Intellectual Origins of the Constitution.* Lawrence: University Press of Kansas, 1985.

————. *We the People: The Economic Origins of the Constitution*. Chicago: University of Chicago Press, 1962.

McGovern, Arthur F. *Liberation Theology and Its Critics: Toward an Assessment*. New York: Orbis Books, 1989.

McLachlan, H. *The Religious Opinions of Milton, Locke and Newton*. Manchester: Manchester University Press, 1941.

McLoughlin, William G. "Enthusiasm for Liberty: The Great Awakening as the Key to the Revolution." In *Preachers and Politics: Two Essays on the Origins of the American Revolution*, by Jack P. Greene and William G. McLoughlin. Worcester, Mass.: American Antiquarian Society, 1977.

McNeill, John T. *The History and Character of Calvinism*. London: Oxford University Press, 1954.

————. "John Calvin on Civil Government." In *Calvinism and the Political Order*, ed. George L. Hunt. Philadelphia: Westminster Press, 1964.

McWilliams, Wilson Carey. "The Bible in the American Political Tradition." In *Religion and Politics*, ed. Myron J. Aronoff. New Brunswick, N.J.: Transaction Books, 1984.

————. *The Idea of Fraternity in America*. Berkeley: University of California Press, 1973.

Mead, Sidney E. *The Lively Experiment: The Shaping of Christianity in America*. New York: Harper and Row, 1963.

————. *Nathaniel William Taylor 1786–1858: A Connecticut Liberal*. Chicago: University of Chicago Press, 1942.

Merquior, J. G. *Liberalism: Old and New*. Boston: G. K. Hall and Co., Twayne Publishers, 1991.

Miller, Perry. *Errand into the Wilderness*. Cambridge: Harvard University Press, Belknap Press, 1984.

————. "The Insecurity of Nature: Being the Dudlian Lecture for the Academic Year 1952–1953 Harvard University." *Harvard Divinity School Bulletin* 19 (1954) 23–38.

————. *Jonathan Edwards*. New York: Meridian Books, 1959.

————. *The New England Mind: From Colony to Province*. Cambridge: Harvard University Press, Belknap Press, 1953.

————. *The New England Mind: The Seventeenth Century*. New York: Macmillan Co., 1939.

————. *Orthodoxy in Massachusetts 1630–1650*. Boston: Beacon Press; Harvard University Press, 1933.

Miller, Perry, Robert L. Calhoun, Nathan M. Pusey, and Reinhold Niebuhr. *Religion and Freedom of Thought*. Freeport, N.Y.: Books for Libraries Press, 1954; repr., n.p.: Doubleday and Co., 1971.

Miller, William Lee. *The First Liberty: Religion and the American Republic.* New York: Alfred A. Knopf, 1986.

Mitchell, Joshua. *Not by Reason Alone: Religion, History, and Identity in Early Modern Political Thought.* Chicago: University of Chicago Press, 1993.

Morgan, Edmund S. *The Birth of the Republic 1763–89.* 3d. ed. Chicago: University of Chicago Press, 1992.

———. *The Gentle Puritan: A Life of Ezra Stiles, 1727–1795.* New Haven: Yale University Press, 1962.

———. *Inventing the People: The Rise of Popular Sovereignty in England and America.* New York: W. W. Norton, 1988.

———. *The Puritan Dilemma: The Story of John Winthrop.* Glenview, Ill.: Scott, Foresman, and Co., 1958.

———. *The Puritan Family: Religion and Domestic Relations in Seventeenth-Century New England.* New York: Harper and Row, 1966.

———. *Visible Saints: The History of a Puritan Idea.* Ithaca: Cornell University Press, 1963.

Morison, Samuel Eliot. *The Founding of Harvard College.* Cambridge: Harvard University Press, 1935.

———. *The Intellectual Life of Colonial New England.* New York: New York University Press, 1956.

———. *Three Centuries of Harvard, 1636–1936.* Cambridge: Harvard University Press, Belknap Press, 1936.

Mouw, Richard J. *The God Who Commands.* Notre Dame: University of Notre Dame Press, 1990.

Murray, John Courtney. *We Hold These Truths: Catholic Reflections on the American Proposition.* Kansas City, Mo.: Sheed and Ward, 1988.

Myers, Minor, Jr. "A Source for Eighteenth-Century Harvard Master's Questions." *William and Mary Quarterly* 38 (April 1981): 261–67.

Neuhaus, Richard John. *The Naked Public Square: Religion and Democracy in America.* 2d ed. Grand Rapids, Mich.: William B. Eerdmans, 1986.

Newlin, Claude M. *Philosophy and Religion in Colonial America.* Westport, Conn.: Greenwood Press, 1971.

Noll, Mark A. *Christians in the American Revolution.* Washington D.C.: Christian University Press, 1977.

———. *Princeton and the Republic, 1768–1822: The Search for a Christian Enlightenment in the Era of Samuel Stanhope Smith.* Princeton: Princeton University Press, 1989.

———, ed. *Religion and American Politics: From the Colonial Period to the 1980s.* New York: Oxford University Press, 1990.

Noll, Mark A., Nathan O. Hatch, and George M. Marsden. *The Search for Christian America.* Westchester, Ill.: Crossway Books, 1983.

Pahl, Jon. *Paradox Lost: Free Will and Political Liberty in American Culture, 1630–1760.* New Studies in American Intellectual and Cultural History, ser. ed. Thomas Bender. Baltimore: Johns Hopkins University Press, 1992.

Pangle, Thomas L. *The Spirit of Modern Republicanism: The Moral Vision of the American Founders and the Philosophy of Locke.* Chicago: University of Chicago Press, 1988.

Patterson, Stephen E. *Political Parties in Revolutionary Massachusetts.* Madison: University of Wisconsin Press, 1973.

Perry, Ralph Barton. *Puritanism and Democracy.* New York: Vanguard Press, 1944.

Pocock, J. G. A. *The Machiavellian Moment: Florentine Political Thought and the Atlantic Republican Tradition.* Princeton: Princeton University Press, 1975.

————. *Politics, Language, and Time: Essays on Political Thought and History.* New York: Atheneum, 1973.

————. "Radical Criticisms of the Whig Order in the Age between Revolutions." In *The Origins of Anglo-American Radicalism,* ed. Margaret Jacob and James Jacob, 33–57. London: George Allen and Unwin, 1984.

————. *Virtue, Commerce, and History: Essays on Political Thought and History, Chiefly in the Eighteenth Century.* Cambridge: Cambridge University Press, 1988.

Puglisi, Michael J. *Puritans Besieged: The Legacies of King Philip's War in the Massachusetts Bay Colony.* Lanham, Md.: University Press of America, 1991.

Rabieh, Michael S. "The Reasonableness of Locke, or the Questionableness of Christianity." *Journal of Politics* 53 (November 1991): 933–57.

Rahe, Paul A. *Republics Ancient and Modern.* Chapel Hill: University of North Carolina Press, 1992.

Rand, Benjamin. "Philosophical Instruction in Harvard University from 1636 to 1900." *Harvard Graduates Magazine* (September 1928): 29–47.

Reid, W. Stanford. *John Calvin: His Influence in the Western World.* Grand Rapids, Mich.: Zondervan Publishing House, 1982.

Reilly, Elizabeth Carroll. "The Wages of Piety: The Boston Book Trade of Jeremy Condy." In *Printing and Society in Early America,* ed. William Leonard Joyce, et al. Worcester, Mass.: American Antiquarian Society, 1983.

Reventlow, Henning Graf. *The Authority of the Bible and the Rise of the Modern World*. Trans. John Bowden. Philadelphia: Fortress Press, 1985.

Robbins, Carolyn. *The Eighteenth-Century Commonwealthsman: Studies in the Transmission, Development, and Circumstance of English Liberal Thought from the Restoration of Charles II until the War with the Thirteen Colonies*. Cambridge: Harvard University Press, 1959.

Robson, David W. *Educating Republicans: The College in the Era of the Revolution, 1750–1800*. Westport, Conn.: Greenwood Press, 1985.

Rosenblum, Nancy L., ed. *Liberalism and the Moral Life*. Cambridge: Harvard University Press, 1989.

Rossiter, Clinton. *Seedtime of the Republic: The Origin of the American Tradition of Political Liberty*. New York: Harcourt, Brace and Co., 1953.

Sandoz, Ellis. *A Government of Laws: Political Theory, Religion, and the American Founding*. Baton Rouge: Louisiana State University Press, 1990.

Scott, Donald M. *From Office to Profession: The New England Ministry, 1750–1850*. N.p.: University of Pennsylvania Press, 1978.

Seybolt, Robert F. "Student Liberties at Harvard, 1763–1764." *Colonial Society of Massachusetts Publications* 28 (April 1933): 449–61.

Shain, Barry Alan. *The Myth of American Individualism: The Protestant Origins of American Political Thought*. Princeton: Princeton University Press, 1994.

Shalhope, Robert E. "Republicanism and Early American Historiography." *William and Mary Quarterly* 39 (April 1982): 334–56.

———. "Toward a Republican Synthesis: The Emergence of an Understanding of Republicanism in American Historiography." *William and Mary Quarterly* 29 (January 1972): 49–80.

Sheldon, Garrett Ward. *The Political Philosophy of Thomas Jefferson*. Baltimore: Johns Hopkins University Press, 1991.

Sheppard, Gerald T. "The Geneva Bible and English Commentary, 1600–1645." In *The Geneva Bible*. Cleveland: Pilgrim Press, 1989.

Shipton, Clifford K. *Sibley's Harvard Graduates: Biographical Sketches of Those Who Attended Harvard College*. Vols. 4–16. Cambridge: Harvard University Press, 1932–1972.

Sibley, John L. *Biographical Sketches of Graduates of Harvard University* Vols. 1–4. Cambridge: Harvard University Press, 1873–1933.

Siegel, Thomas Jay. "Governance and Curriculum at Harvard College in the Eighteenth Century." Ph.D. diss., Harvard University, 1990.

Sinopoli, Richard C. *The Foundations of American Citizenship: Liberalism, the Constitution, and Civic Virtue*. New York: Oxford University Press, 1992.

Skillen, James William. "The Development of Calvinistic Political Theory in the Netherlands, with Special Reference to the Thought of Herman Dooyeweerd." Ph.D. diss., Duke University, 1973.

Skinner, Quentin. *The Foundations of Modern Political Thought.* 2 vols. Cambridge: Cambridge University Press, 1978.

Sperry, Willard L. *Religion in America.* Boston: Beacon Press, 1963.

Stimson, Shannon C. *The American Revolution in the Law: Anglo-American Jurisprudence before John Marshall.* Princeton: Princeton University Press, 1990.

Stoner, James R., Jr. *Common Law and Liberal Theory: Coke, Hobbes, and the Origins of American Constitutionalism.* Lawrence: University Press of Kansas, 1992.

Stout, Harry S. *The New England Soul: Preaching and Religious Culture in Colonial New England.* New York: Oxford University Press, 1986.

Strauss, Leo. *Natural Right and History.* Chicago: University of Chicago Press, 1953.

Sullivan, William M. *Reconstructing Public Philosophy.* Berkeley: University of California Press, 1986.

Swift, Lindsay. "The Massachusetts Election Sermons." *The Colonial Society of Massachusetts* 1 (December 1894): 388–451.

Toulouse, Teresa. *The Art of Prophesying: New England Sermons and the Shaping of Belief.* Athens: University of Georgia Press, 1987.

Vail, R. W. G. *A Check List of New England Sermons.* Worcester, Mass.: [American Antiquarian] Society, 1936.

Van Tyne, Claude H. *The Causes of the War of Independence. . . .* Boston: Houghton Mifflin, 1922.

———. "Influence of the Clergy, and of Religious and Sectarian Forces, on the American Revolution." *American Historical Review* 29 (1913–1914): 44–64.

Walker, Williston. *A History of the Congregational Churches in the United States.* New York: Christian Literature Co., 1894.

Walzer, Michael. *The Revolution of the Saints: A Study in the Origin of Radical Politics.* New York: Atheneum, 1974.

Weber, Donald. *Rhetoric and History in Revolutionary New England.* New York: Oxford University Press, 1988.

Weis, Frederick Lewis. *The Colonial Clergy and the Colonial Churches of New England.* Baltimore: Genealogical Publishing Co., 1977.

Wells, Ronald A., and Thomas A. Askew, eds. *Liberty and Law: Reflections on the Constitution in American Life and Thought.* Grand Rapids, Mich.: William B. Eerdmans, 1987.

Wentz, Richard E. *Religion in the New World: The Shaping of Religious Traditions in the United States.* Minneapolis: Fortress Press, 1990.

Whitehead, John W. *The Second American Revolution.* Elgin, Ill.: David C. Cook, 1983.

Williams, George Huniston. "Translatio Studii: The Puritans' Conception of Their First University in New England, 1636." *Archive for Reformation History* 57, nos. 1–2 (1966): 152–81.

Wills, Garry. *Explaining America: The Federalist.* New York: Penguin Books, 1981.

———. *Inventing America: Jefferson's Declaration of Independence.* New York: Random House, Vintage Books, 1979.

Withington, Ann Fairfax, *Toward a More Perfect Union: Virtue and the Formation of American Republics.* New York: Oxford University Press, 1991.

Witte, John, Jr. "How to Govern a City on a Hill: The Early Puritan Contribution to American Constitutionalism." *Emory Law Journal* 39 (Winter 1990): 41–64.

Wolff, Robert Paul. *The Poverty of Liberalism.* Boston: Beacon Press, 1968.

Wood, Gordon S. *The Creation of the American Republic, 1776–1787.* New York: W. W. Norton, 1969.

———. *The Radicalism of the American Revolution.* New York: Alfred A. Knopf, 1992.

———. "The Virtues and the Interests." Review of *Republicanism and Bourgeois Radicalism: Political Ideology in Late Eighteenth-Century England and America,* by Isaac Kramnick. *New Republic,* February 11, 1991, 32–35.

Worthley, Harold Field. "An Historical Essay: The Massachusetts Convention of Congregational Ministers." *Proceedings of the Unitarian Historical Society* 12 (1958): 47–103.

Wright, Conrad. *The Beginnings of Unitarianism in America.* N.p.: Starr King Press, 1955.

Yolton, John W. *Locke: An Introduction.* New York: Basil Blackwell, 1985.

———, ed. *John Locke: Problems and Perspectives: A Collection of New Essays.* Cambridge: Cambridge University Press, 1969.

INDEX

CREDITS

Acknowledgment is made as follows for permission to quote from copyrighted material:

Passages from *The New England Clergy and the American Revolution,* by Alice M. Baldwin, copyright © 1928, by Duke University Press, Durham, N.C., and reprinted with permission.

Passages from *Errand into the Wilderness* by Perry Miller, Cambridge, Mass.: The Belknap Press of Harvard University Press, copyright © 1956 by the President and Fellows of Harvard College, and used by permission.

Quotation of remarks made by Professor John Dunn, King's College, Cambridge, during an interview with the author on May 27, 1992, in Cambridge, England, and used by permission.

Passages from *A Preface to American Political Theory* by Donald S. Lutz, copyright © 1992 University Press of Kansas, and reprinted with permission.

Passages from *The New England Soul: Preaching and Religious Culture in Colonial New England* by Harry S. Stout, copyright © 1986 by Oxford University Press, and reprinted with permission.